097594

Edinhurgh

OLEG LLANDRILLO CYM
O FAN ADNODDAU
RESOURCE
0149
DIRECTIONS

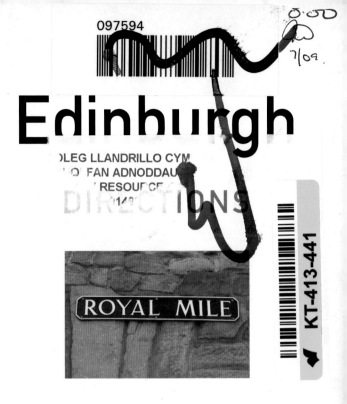

ROYAL MILE

KT-413-441

WRITTEN AND RESEARCHED BY

Donald Reid

**ROUGH
GUIDES**

NEW YORK • LONDON • DELHI
www.roughguides.com

Contents

Introduction	4

Ideas	9
The big six	10
Edinburgh Festival	12
Royal Edinburgh	14
A taste of Edinburgh	16
Theatre and music	18
Medieval Edinburgh	20
Dead Edinburgh	22
Literary Edinburgh	24
Galleries and museums	26
Sports and activities	28
Traditional pubs	30
Classical Edinburgh	32
Restaurants and cafés	34
Secret Edinburgh	36
Gourmet Edinburgh	38
Clubs and bars	40
Gay Edinburgh	42
Indulgent Edinburgh	44
Festivals and events	46
Green places	48
Edinburgh views	50
Kids' Edinburgh	52
Modern architecture	54
Eccentric Edinburgh	56
Shopping	58
Nautical Edinburgh	60
Art outdoors	62

Places	65
The Royal Mile	67
Holyrood and Arthur's Seat	82
South of the Royal Mile	90
Along Princes Street	102
The New Town	110
Calton Hill and Broughton	119
Along the Water of Leith	126
Leith	133
North and west Edinburgh	139
South Edinburgh	145
South Queensferry and the Forth Bridges	151

Accommodation	157
Hotels, self-catering apartments, guesthouses and B&Bs	159
Hostels	167

Essentials	169
Arrival and getting around	171
Information	172
Entertainment	173
The Edinburgh Festival	176
Events calendar	180
Directory	181

Index	188

Introduction to

Edinburgh

Laid out over a series of volcanic hills and with its jagged skyline topped by the craggy castle, few European cities can boast Edinburgh's dramatic impact. The cobbled medieval closes, steep stairways and hidden courtyards of the labyrinthine Old Town, along with the wide thoroughfares and grand Neoclassical facades of the eighteenth-century New Town, together constitute a World Heritage Site – a historic treasure that's also the heart of the living, working city.

With everything from tightly packed tenement houses to faux Venetian palaces and dynamic contemporary constructions, Edinburgh is a compellingly theatrical place – awash with history yet refreshingly modern, and as thick with pomp and grandeur as it is intimate and friendly. Its centre is remarkably compact, and the majority of the main sights are within easy walking distance of each other. The city is also characterized by extensive green spaces: you can climb to the top of Arthur's Seat to look over Edinburgh and its suburbs, walk along the verdant Water of Leith, or stand by

When to visit

Edinburgh's typically British climate means a clear seasonal divide between frost- and snow-tinged winters, blustery and colourful springs, warm (but rarely hot) summers and golden, then gloomy, autumns. The east coast location ensures slightly less rainfall than western Scotland, though sharp and sometimes bitter winds blow in off the North Sea. The coldest months are January and February, with an average daily temperature of 6°C; in July the average is 18°C; late spring (May) and early autumn (September) are often good times to visit, offering welcome spells of bright weather and less of the high season's tourist scrum. With the Festival in full swing, August is perhaps *the* most exciting time to be in Edinburgh, though be prepared for huge crowds.

▲ Edinburgh cityscape

the breezy shores of the Firth of Forth and admire the gigantic geometric girders of the Forth Rail Bridge.

Edinburgh's status as Scottish capital has endowed it with an outstanding collection of national institutions, from museums and magnificent art collections to a controversial but intriguing new parliament building, as well as a host of more populist attractions that include a high-tech science centre and the world's best indoor climbing facility. And while the city is rich in heritage, it's also confident in its role as a thoroughly modern European capital. The prevailing

▼ Fringe posters

◄ Old Town

◄ Buskers, Royal Mile

conservatism is cast aside both in the flair of the annual Festival, which transforms Edinburgh into a giant celebration of the arts and entertainment, and in the hedonism of the New Year party, Hogmanay, when thousands of revellers throng the streets and the skies explode with fireworks. Theatres, live-music venues and art galleries provide rich cultural pickings throughout the year, while the old wood-lined pubs, cosmopolitan cafés and clubs, dramatic rooftop restaurants and busy seafood bistros provide all the evidence you need of a city charged with spirit and life among its old stones.

Edinburgh
AT A GLANCE

Leith

The port of Edinburgh, Leith is just as historic as the city – if rather less well preserved and fringed by some grim housing estates. The old harbour, however, now holds some fine seafood restaurants, while the redeveloped former docklands are the retirement home of that epitome of the British establishment, the Royal Yacht *Britannia*.

◄ Leith

◄ Water of Leith

Water of Leith

Little more than a meandering stream, the Water of Leith threads its way through the suburbs in the north of the city, with an accompanying walkway offering a verdant, leafy passage between non-touristy districts such as Stockbridge, Inverleith and Dean Village.

New Town

A masterpiece of early town planning, with row upon elegant row of impressive Georgian houses intermixed with haughty Neoclassical monuments, the New Town's oldest quarter has been colonized by department stores and offices. Explore further and you'll discover attractive residential enclaves as well as bohemian Broughton, the focus of Edinburgh's gay scene.

◄ New Town

Old Town

This is the core of historic Edinburgh, with the centrepiece Royal Mile and its string of key attractions running east from the castle down to Holyrood, home of the royal palace and brand-new parliament. The tangled passageways and courtyards which lead off the Mile are far less touristy, and remain evocative of the area's medieval character.

Holyrood Park

Just half a mile from the city centre, this vast public park covers as large an area as the Old and New Towns combined. Mostly made up of rough, hilly terrain that offers some terrific walks, it incorporates the 823-foot peak of Arthur's Seat as well as the striking Salisbury Crags cliffs.

▲ Holyrood Park

Ideas

The big six

Part of the pleasure of visiting Edinburgh is in simply wandering with no fixed agenda, through narrow closes and up vertiginous steps, or along the grand avenues of the New Town. But there are some landmark sights that you really shouldn't miss. These encapsulate what's great about Scotland's capital, where history, heritage and dramatic views mix with impressive buildings from many eras, including a number of dynamic modern constructions.

▲ Calton Hill

Studded with a bizarre collection of Neoclassical architecture, this is the best of many great viewpoints from which to gaze out over the city.

P.119 ▶ CALTON HILL AND BROUGHTON

▲ Forth Rail Bridge

The gigantic girders of this iconic monument to Victorian engineering span the Firth of Forth just north of Edinburgh.

P.154 ▶ SOUTH QUEENSFERRY AND THE FORTH BRIDGES

Essentials

Arrival and getting around

City transport

Although Edinburgh occupies a large area relative to its population, most places worth visiting lie within the compact city centre, which is easily explored on foot. To get to the suburbs, however, or to travel across the central area, the local **public transport** system is a relatively simple and efficient option, with most services terminating on or near Princes Street. The city is generally well served by **buses**; most useful are the white and maroon ones operated by **Lothian Buses** (⊛ www.lothianbuses.co.uk), which provide the most frequent and comprehensive coverage of the city. Usefully, every bus stop displays diagrams indicating which services pass the stop and which routes they take. Lothian Buses timetables and passes are available from their ticket centres on Waverley Bridge, Shandwick Place or 27 Hanover Street (see the map on p.103; enquiry line ⊕ 0131/555 6363). A good investment, especially if you're staying away from the centre or want to explore the suburbs, is the £12 "Ridacard" bus pass allowing a week's unlimited travel on Lothian services. Lothian also offer a LRT day pass allowing unlimited travel for £2.50 (£2 if you buy it after 9.30am or at weekends). Tickets are also available from drivers; you'll need exact change, and the most common fare is 80p. The predominantly white, single-decker buses of **First Edinburgh** (⊕ 0870/872 7271; ⊛ www.firstgroup.com) also cover a number of the main routes through town, but are better for outlying towns and villages. They have their own system of tickets and day-tickets, similar in structure to Lothian Buses; for travel within the city,

is at Turnhouse, seven miles west of the city centre close to the start of the M8 motorway to Glasgow. Airlink shuttle buses (#100) connect to Waverley railway station in the centre of town in just under half an hour; they run 24 hours a day, with services departing every ten or twenty minutes between 5am and midnight, then hourly through the night (£3 single). Lothian bus #35 runs (daytime only every 20–30mins; £1) from the airport to the west of Edinburgh, the Royal Mile and Leith, but takes significantly longer. Taxis charge £15–20 from the airport into the town centre.

Situated right at the heart of the city between Princes Street and the Royal Mile, **Waverley Station** (⊕ 0845/748 4950; ⊛ www.nationalrail.co.uk) is the terminus for all mainline trains. Most services from England are run by GNER (⊕ 0845/722 5225; ⊛ www.gner.co.uk) or Virgin Trains (⊕ 0845/722 2333; ⊛ www.virgintrains. co.uk); sleeper services from London and all services within Scotland are operated by First ScotRail (⊕ 0845/755 0033; ⊛ www.scotrail.co.uk). There's a rank for black taxis within the station, while buses to all parts of town leave from the adjacent streets. There's a second mainline train stop, **Haymarket Station**, just under two miles west on the lines from Waverley to Glasgow, Fife and the Highlands, although this is only really of use if you're staying nearby.

The **coach** terminal for local and inter-city services is on St Andrew Square, two minutes' walk from Waverley Station on the opposite side of Princes Street.

Run by Superfast (⊕ 0870/234 0870; ⊛ www.superfast.com), daily **ferries** from Zeebrugge in Belgium dock at Rosyth, not far from the Forth Road Bridge to the

Edinburgh International Airport (⊕ 0870/040 0007; ⊛ www.baa.com)

northwest of Edinburgh. Bus #X2 runs into town from here (£3).

the standard fare is 80p, with unlimited day travel for £2.30 (£1.80 after 9.30am). Most services depart from and terminate at or near St Andrew Square, where the main **bus and coach station** is located, or Waterloo Place, the eastern extension of Princes Street.

The city is well endowed with **taxi** ranks, and you can also hail black cabs on the street. Costs are reasonable – you'll pay around £6 from the city centre to Leith, for example. If you want to call a taxi, try any one of the following: Computer Cabs ☎ 0131/228 2555; Central Radio Taxis ☎ 0131/229 2468; or City Cabs ☎ 0131/228 1211.

Edinburgh has almost no suburban **rail** services; the one main place of interest served by trains is South Queensferry, while all mainline services to Fife, Inverness and Aberdeen stop at Dalmeny station (see p.000).

Tours

Open-top **bus tours** are big business in Edinburgh, with three rival companies taking largely similar routes around the main sights. All depart from Waverley Bridge and all allow you to get on and off at leisure. The most entertaining of

the three are MacTours (☎ 0131/556 2244, ⊛ www.mactours.co.uk), which use a fleet of characterful vintage buses. Most of the **walking tours** are based on and around the Royal Mile; for more on these, see p.000. Elsewhere in the city, Geowalks (☎ 0131/555 5488, ⊛ www.geowalks.demon.co.uk), offers guided walks up Arthur's Seat in the company of a qualified geologist; Rebustours (☎ 07866/536752, ⊛ www.rebustours.com) trace the footsteps of Inspector Rebus, hero of Ian Rankin's bestselling detective novels; while the city tours offered by Leith Walks (☎ 0131/555 2500, ⊛ www.leithwalks.co.uk) include a *Trainspotting* tour of some of the scenes famous from Irvine Welsh's novels. Adrian's Edinburgh City Cycle Tour (☎ 07966/477206, ⊛ www.edinburghcycletour.com) uses peddle-power for an enjoyable and good-value three-hour Edinburgh tour, with all equipment provided. If you want a break from the city, Walkabout Scotland (☎ 0131/661 7168, ⊛ www.walkaboutscotland.com) will pick you up from the city centre and whisk you off on a one-day walking trip in the Highlands. Prices range from £7–8 for walking tours to £15 for the cycle tour and £40 for a Walkabout Scotland day-trip.

Information

Edinburgh's main **tourist office** is on top of Princes Mall near the northern entrance to Waverley station (April & Oct Mon–Sat 9am–6pm, Sun 10am–6pm; May, June & Sept Mon–Sat 9am–7pm, Sun 10am–7pm; July & Aug Mon–Sat 9am–8pm, Sun 10am–8pm; Nov–March Mon–Wed 9am–5pm, Thurs–Sat 9am–6pm, Sun 10am–5pm; ☎ 0845/225 5121, ⊛ www.edinburgh.org). Although inevitably hectic at the height of the season, it's reasonably efficient, with scores of free leaflets and a bank of computers available if you want to search for information on the web (£1

for 20mins). The much smaller **airport branch** is in the main concourse, directly opposite Gate 5 (daily: April–Oct 6.30am–10.30pm, Nov–March 7am–9pm).

The best guide to local events is *The List* (£2.20), available fortnightly from newsagents; more suggestions for finding out what's on are given on p.173.

Websites

⊛ **www.edinburgh.org** Edinburgh and Lothian tourist board site, with a wealth of local info and an online accommodation booking service.

▼ The Royal Mile

One of the world's most famous streets, with every cobbled inch resonant with history and atmosphere.

P.67 ▶ THE ROYAL MILE

▲ National Museum of Scotland

This impressive piece of contemporary design is a worthy home for Scotland's national historic treasures.

P.93 ▶ SOUTH OF THE ROYAL MILE

▼ Edinburgh Castle

This mighty historic fortress, perched atop its impregnable rock, is compelling from all angles as well as from within.

P.67 ▶ THE ROYAL MILE

▲ Scottish Parliament

Overflowing with imagery, quirky design and controversy, and now one of the city's star attractions.

P.84 ▶ HOLYROOD AND ARTHUR'S SEAT

Edinburgh Festival

The Edinburgh Festival is one of the greatest shows on earth, a month of cultural gluttony and mind-boggling artistic activity. Every performance space – from the grandest concert halls to pub courtyards – plays host to a packed programme of arts and entertainment, ranging from orchestral performances to stand-up comedy, ground-breaking theatre to avant-garde cinema. Whether you're dashing around a dozen shows in a day or checking out the street performers, Edinburgh in August is an essential experience.

▼ Fireworks concert

This spectacular and free Festival climax lights up the night sky above the castle.

P.177 ▶ ESSENTIALS

▼ International Festival

This highbrow event draws world-class orchestras, choirs, dance and theatre companies to Edinburgh.

P.176 ▶ ESSENTIALS

▼ The Fringe

Posters, flyers and leaflets plaster the city's walls, windows and lampposts advertising the Fringe's 1500 daily shows.

P.177 ▶ ESSENTIALS

▲ Street theatre

During the Festival the Royal Mile becomes one elongated stage.

P.176 ▶ ESSENTIALS

▼ Edinburgh International Book Festival

This hugely popular fortnight features readings, discussions and interviews with well-known authors.

P.178 ▶ ESSENTIALS

▲ Comedy

A successful Fringe stand-up show is the benchmark of success for almost every comedian in Britain.

P.177 ▶ ESSENTIALS

Royal Edinburgh

The monarch need not be at her official Edinburgh residence for the capital to adopt the trappings of a royal city. The lives of the Stewarts (six kings named James, plus Mary, Queen of Scots) were intricately involved with Edinburgh for centuries – it was from Holyrood that James VI departed for London to unite the thrones of Britain. Today, the Castle secures Scotland's crown jewels and coronation stone, while Leith harbours that most quintessential emblem of the British royalty abroad, the Royal Yacht *Britannia*.

▲ Edinburgh Castle

The castle's permanent military garrison help guard the "Honours", or crown jewels, of Scotland.

P.67 ▸ THE ROYAL MILE

▼ Queen's Gallery

Precious art and artefacts from the rarely seen Royal Collection are displayed in this attractive new gallery at Holyrood.

P.83 ▸ HOLYROOD AND ARTHUR'S SEAT

▲ Thistle Chapel, High Kirk of St Giles

This beautiful side-chapel is used by the Queen to install Knights of the Thistle, the highest chivalric order in Scotland.

P.73 ▸ THE ROYAL MILE

▼ Royal Yacht Britannia

Now enjoying dignified retirement in Leith, *Britannia* offers an intriguing insight into Britain's recent royal heritage.

P.135 ▸ LEITH

▲ Palace of Holyroodhouse

An impressive introduction into the lives and loves of the Scottish kings and queens.

P.82 ▸ HOLYROOD AND ARTHUR'S SEAT

A taste of Edinburgh

Scottish food has a somewhat unfortunate reputation, the locals' predilection for deep fried suppers and sugar-packed delicacies overshadowing the undoubted quality of the country's seafood, meat, game and soft fruit. In Edinburgh you can try both, from lip-smacking fast food to exquisitely prepared modern Scottish cuisine. The home-grown favourite among soft drinks is the rust-coloured Irn Bru, while if you've a taste for the harder stuff look for the excellent selection of locally produced beers and smooth malt whisky.

▼ Irn Bru

It's sweet, sticky and it's bright orange, yet Irn Bru is the nation's favourite fizzy drink: you'll find it on sale all over town.

P.149 ▸ SOUTH EDINBURGH

▼ Modern Scottish cuisine

Edinburgh's top chefs are adept at using Scottish produce such as Aberdeen Angus at the heart of their most inspired culinary creations.

P.80 ▸ THE ROYAL MILE

▲ Pint of 80/-

Eighty shilling ale, or "heavy", is a traditional Scots beer, brown in colour but sweeter and smoother than English bitter.

P.101 ▸ SOUTH OF THE ROYAL MILE

▲ Fish and chips

When it comes to fast food, there's nothing more satisfying than a fish supper.

P.79 ▸ THE ROYAL MILE

▼ Luca's ice cream

The Scots' sweet tooth has ensured a discerning taste for ice cream – the local favourite by far is Luca's creamy vanilla.

P.149 ▸ SOUTH EDINBURGH

▼ Glenkinchie whisky

Known as "the lowland malt", Glenkinchie is an easy-drinking single malt whisky made in East Lothian, just outside Edinburgh.

P.70 ▸ THE ROYAL MILE

Theatre and music

Thankfully, Edinburgh's cultural life doesn't shut down for the eleven months of the year that the city spends recovering from the festival. An array of excellent venues, some serious local talent and a deeply embedded appreciation of music, song and performance combine to ensure an impressive variety of theatre and music across the city year-round, from touring performances of the Royal Shakespeare Company to an impromptu folk or jazz session.

▲ Henry's Jazz Bar

This atmospheric basement venue hosts Edinburgh's most consistent lineup of local and touring jazz acts.

P.174 ▸ ESSENTIALS

▼ Usher Hall

The city's dignified old concert hall hosts the world's top orchestras as well as big-name rock and pop acts.

P.174 ▶ ESSENTIALS

▼ Festival Theatre

The prime place in town for national and international ballet and opera performances.

P.175 ▶ ESSENTIALS

▲ Sandy Bell's

A small traditional pub, where friends with fiddles tend to meet – and invariably strike up a tune or two.

P.174 ▶ ESSENTIALS

▲ Traverse Theatre

Consistently impressive, staging ground-breaking new writing and innovative contemporary drama.

P.175 ▶ ESSENTIALS

Medieval Edinburgh

Few European capitals have preserved the medieval era so resonantly as Edinburgh, in grand buildings such as the High Kirk of St Giles and ruined Holyrood Abbey, and in the haphazard layout of the Old Town itself. With its narrow passageways off the Royal Mile leading to tightly packed tenement houses which rise a giddying eight or nine storeys, a wander through the cobbled streets here can take you straight back through the centuries.

▼ Holyrood Abbey

These atmospheric remains are a poignant memorial to the destructive religious wars which dominated medieval Scotland.

P.83 ▸ HOLYROOD AND ARTHUR'S SEAT

▼ Canongate Kirk

This gracefully simple seventeenth-century church boasts the city's most attractive historic graveyard.

P.76 ▸ THE ROYAL MILE

▲ Grassmarket and Victoria Street

Tall tenements crowd around this rough-and-tumble Old Town quarter, notable for its quirky shops and friendly pubs.

P.90 ▸ SOUTH OF THE ROYAL MILE

▲ Inchcolm

This tranquil island holds Scotland's finest original medieval abbey, and affords sweeping views back to Edinburgh.

P.154 ▸ SOUTH QUEENSFERRY
AND THE FORTH BRIDGES

▼ Parliament Square

The symbolic heart of the Old Town is dominated by the distinctive fifteenth-century crown spire of the High Kirk of St Giles.

P.72 ▸ THE ROYAL MILE

▼ Gladstone's Land

The best preserved of the Royal Mile's tenements, this creaking, dark building gives a glimpse of medieval life in the city.

P.71 ▸ THE ROYAL MILE

Dead Edinburgh

There's a distinctly sinister and macabre edge to Edinburgh's history, and if you join a tour of the old cemeteries or walk through the narrow corridors of the Old Town after dusk, you're bound to absorb some of this rather creepy atmosphere. The dead are given life here in less spooky ways, too, whether through the legions of visitors who research the details of long-forgotten ancestors at Edinburgh's archives, or by having a few drinks by the site of the city's old gallows.

▲ Surgeon's Hall Museum

A wonderfully macabre museum dedicated to surgery, anatomy and pathology.

P.96 ▸ SOUTH OF THE ROYAL MILE

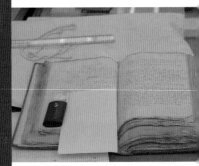

▲ Ancestor research

Clamber around your family tree via the extensive resources of the General Register Office, the National Archives of Scotland and the National Library.

P.102 ▸ ALONG PRINCES STREET

Entertainment

Inevitably, Edinburgh's entertainment scene is at its best during the Festival (see p.176), which can make the other 49 weeks of the year seem like a bit of an anticlimax. The city does have plenty to offer throughout the year, however, especially in the realm of theatre and music.

The best way to find out what's on is to pick up a copy of *The List* (see p.172). Alternatively, get hold of the *Edinburgh Evening News* (Mon–Sat): its listings column gives details of performances in the city that day, including those at hotels and bars. For information on nightclubs, you can also check out the posters and piles of flyers distributed to most of the pre-club bars around town. Box offices of individual halls and theatres are likewise liberally supplied with promotional leaflets about forthcoming music and theatre, and some are able to sell tickets for more than one venue.

Nightclubs

The Bongo Club 37 Holyrood Rd, Old Town ☎0131/558 7604, ⊛ www.thebongoclub.co.uk. Daily till 3am. Legendary Edinburgh club that attracts some of the most interesting DJs around. Look out for the mighty Messenger Sound System pumping out reggae twice-monthly on Saturdays.

Cabaret Voltaire 36–38 Blair St, Old Town ☎0131/220 6176, ⊛ www.cabaret-voltaire.co.uk. Daily 10.30pm–3am. A nightclub in the atmospheric setting of the Old Town's underground vaults. Head here for some fine R&B and hip-hop at weekends, as well as live acoustic sets in the week.

Ego 14 Picardy Place, Broughton ☎0131/478 7434, Tues–Sat 11pm–3am, Sun & Mon reserved for private parties/special events. A former casino, this big venue hosts Wiggle, which plays to a gay and mixed crowd monthly on the third Saturday of every month, and the epic party night Vegas on the first or second Saturday. The smaller *Cocteau Lounge* downstairs is occasionally in use for more intimate and sophisticated club nights.

Honeycomb 15–17 Niddrie St, Old Town ☎0131/556 2442, ⊛ www.the-honeycomb.com. Tues–Sat 11pm–3am. In amongst the vaults and hidden passageways under the Old Town, the main attractions at this much

⊛ www.edinburgh.gov.uk This Edinburgh City Council site gives the lowdown on local services, from transport to kids' facilities, and has lots of links.

⊛ www.edinburghfestivals.co.uk A good gateway into all Edinburgh's major festivals, including the Fringe, Film Festival and Hogmanay.

⊛ www.theoracle.co.uk Useful what's-on site with comprehensive listings.

⊛ www.edinburghj247.com Decent general site with news, events listings, weather and links.

⊛ www.edinburghguide.com Good links directory covering everything from entertainment to education; decent listings for theatre and cinema, too.

⊛ www.kidsedinburgh.com Searchable database that offers ideas and suggestions for places to visit and events for different age groups.

⊛ www.edinburgh-galleries.co.uk This well-maintained site details exhibitions taking place at most of Edinburgh's public and private galleries.

⊛ www.edinburgharchitecture.co.uk Attractive site dedicated to the capital's contemporary architecture and design, with photos, suggested tours and details of the coolest restaurants and hotels.

⊛ www.ceolas.org Site specializing in Celtic music, both historical and contemporary, with lots of tunes to listen to.

⊛ www.origins.net A good place to start searching for your long-lost Scottish ancestors, developed in association with the General Register Office of Scotland. Follow the links to "Web Resources" and then to "Gateway to Scotland" for some excellent background information to all things Scottish, and a myriad of links.

⊛ www.rampantscotland.com Excellent links directory, organized by subject, covering all aspects of Scotland.

admired venue include big drum'n'bass night Manga, and Bio-Rhythm, which showcases guest DJs from around the UK.

The Liquid Room 9c Victoria St, Old Town ☎0131/225 2564, ⊛www .liquidroom.com. Tues–Sun 10.30pm–3am. One of the best of Edinburgh's larger venues, with nights such as the indie Evol, and Colours, a house/techno club drawing big-name DJs.

Opal Lounge 51 George St, New Town ☎0131/226 2275, ⊛www.opallounge. co.uk. Daily noon–3am. See and be-seen bar in the New Town with DJs funking things up later on. As well as the beautiful people you'll also find office groups lingering on long after their post-work drink.

Gay clubs and bars

CC Blooms 23 Greenside Place, Broughton ☎0131/556 9331. Daily 7pm–3am. Edinburgh's only uniquely gay club, with a big dancefloor, stonking rhythms and a young, friendly crowd.

Planet Out 6 Baxter's Place, Broughton ☎0131/524 0061. Daily 4pm–1am. This loud and outrageous bar beside the Playhouse Theatre operates mostly as a pre-club venue, but it's a popular drinking spot in its own right and is known as the place to meet people.

Sala 60 Broughton St, Broughton ☎0131/478 7069. Tues–Thurs & Sun 11am–11pm, Fri & Sat 11am–1am. Bar food, light snacks and drinks in a relaxed atmosphere at the Edinburgh Gay, Lesbian and Bisexual Centre.

Live music venues

Bannermans 212 Cowgate, Old Town ☎0131/556 3254, ⊛www .bannermansgigs.co.uk. Daily midday–1am. This longstanding pub is the best place in central Edinburgh to discover local indie bands hoping for a big break, with live music every evening but Tuesday.

Corn Exchange 11 Newmarket Rd, Slateford ☎0131/477 3500, ⊛www.ece. uk.com. This rather misleadingly named former slaughterhouse is now a popular 3000-capacity venue for big-name contemporary pop and rock acts, but the location, three miles west of the centre, is a bit off-putting.

Henry's Jazz Bar 8 Morrison St, off Lothian Rd, West End ☎0131/467 5200. Tues–Sun 8.30pm–3am. Edinburgh's premier jazz and hip-hop venue, with

live music every night and regular top performers.

The Liquid Room 9c Victoria St, Old Town ☎0131/225 2528, ⊛www .liquidroom.com. Closed Mon. One of Edinburgh's best mid-sized venues for touring indie and R&B bands; gigs are interspersed with club nights.

Royal Oak 1 Infirmary St, Old Town ☎0131/557 2976, ⊛www.royal-oak -folk.com. Mon–Sat 11am–2am, Sun 12.30pm–2am. A traditional pub hosting regular informal folk sessions and the "Wee Folk Club", featuring gigs by guest performers, on Sundays.

Queen's Hall 89 Clerk St, Newington ☎0131/668 2019, ⊛www.thequeenshall .net. Converted Georgian church which now operates as a concert hall; it's used principally by the Scottish Chamber Orchestra and Scottish Ensemble, as well as touring jazz, blues and folk groups.

Sandy Bell's 25 Forrest Rd, Old Town ☎0131/225 2751. Mon–Sat 11.30am–1am, Sun 12.30–11pm. This friendly bar is a good bet for folk music most nights of the week.

Usher Hall Corner of Lothian Rd and Grindlay St, West End ☎0131/228 1155, ⊛www.usherhall.co.uk. Edinburgh's main civic concert hall, seating over 2500, is excellent for choral and symphony concerts, but less suitable for solo vocalists. The upper circle seats are cheapest and have the best acoustics, but the sound quality overall is much improved after a recent refurbishment.

The Venue 15 Calton Rd, Calton ☎0131/557 3073, ⊛www.edinvenue .com. This small, intimate and sweaty place is used mainly for club nights, but also hosts up-and-coming indie bands.

Whistlebinkies 4–6 South Bridge, Old Town ☎0131/557 5114, ⊛www .whistlebinkies.com. Daily 7pm–3am. One of Edinburgh's most reliable venues for live music every night of the week – often it's rock and pop covers, though there are some folk evenings.

Theatre and dance venues

Assembly Rooms 54 George St, New Town ☎0131/226 2428, ⊛www .assemblyrooms.com. This venerable complex of small and large halls is used all year, but really comes into its own during the Fringe, when large-scale drama productions and mainstream comedy are staged. At other times it's used for shows,

ESSENTIALS | Entertainment

dances and the occasional music event.

Bedlam Theatre 2a Forrest Rd, Old Town ☎ 0131/225 9893, ⊛ www .bedlamtheatre.co.uk. Housed in a converted Victorian church, the Bedlam is used predominantly for student productions of varying quality and impact, but raises its game during the Festival.

Dance Base 14–16 Grassmarket, Old Town ☎ 0131/225 5255, ⊛ www .dancebase.co.uk. Scotland's sparkling new National Centre for Dance is used mostly for modern dance workshops and classes, but also hosts occasional performances.

Festival Theatre Nicolson St, Old Town ☎ 0131/529 6000, ⊛ www.eft.co.uk. The largest stage in Britain, principally used for Scottish Opera and Scottish Ballet's appearances in the capital, as well as for everything from the children's show *Singing Kettle* to Engelbert Humperdinck.

King's Theatre 2 Leven St, Tollcross ☎ 0131/529 6000, ⊛ www.eft.co.uk. Stately Edwardian civic theatre that majors in pantomime, touring West End plays and the occasional major drama or opera performance.

Playhouse Theatre 18–22 Greenside Place, Broughton ☎ 0870/606 3424, ⊛ www.edinburgh-playhouse.co.uk. Recently refurbished, this former cinema is the most capacious theatre in Britain, and plays host to extended runs of popular musicals as well as occasional rock concerts.

Royal Lyceum Theatre 30 Grindlay St, West End ☎ 0131/248 4848, ⊛ www .lyceum.org.uk. This fine Victorian civic theatre, with its compact auditorium, is Edinburgh's leading year-round venue for mainstream drama.

Theatre Workshop 34 Hamilton Place, Stockbridge ☎ 0131/226 5425, ⊛ www .theatre-workshop.com. Enticing programmes of innovative international theatre and performance art. Strong in the Festival and over Christmas, but fewer shows at other times.

Traverse Theatre 10 Cambridge St, West End ☎ 0131/228 1404, ⊛ www.traverse .co.uk. Unquestionably one of Britain's premier venues for new plays and avant-garde drama from around the world, and going from strength to strength in its new custom-built home beside the Usher Hall.

Comedy venues

Jongleurs Omni Centre, Greenside Place ☎ 0870/787 0707, ⊛ www .jongleurs.com. Thurs–Sat 7pm–2am (last entry 9pm). This Edinburgh link in a national chain, located in a huge glass-fronted cinema complex at the foot of Calton Hill, offers a year-round chance to encounter popular Festival stand-up acts and national stars.

The Stand 5 York Place, New Town ☎ 0131/558 7272, ⊛ www.thestand .co.uk. Mon–Sat 12.30pm–1am, Sun 12.30pm–midnight. The city's top comedy spot, with a different act on every night and some of the UK's best comics headlining at the weekends. The bar is worth a visit in itself.

Cinemas

Cameo 38 Home St, Tollcross ☎ 0131/228 4141, ⊛ www.picturehouses .co.uk. A treasure of an arthouse cinema, screening more challenging mainstream releases alongside cult late-nighters.

Dominion 18 Newbattle Terrace, Morningside ☎ 0131/447 4771, ⊛ www .dominioncinema.com. A reminder of how cinemas were before multiplexes, the Dominion is still family-owned, and battling on with its screenings of popular new releases.

Filmhouse 88 Lothian Rd, West End ☎ 0131/228 2688, ⊛ www .filmhousecinema.com. Three screens showing an eclectic programme of independent, arthouse and classic films. The café is chief hangout for the city's film buffs.

Odeon 118 Lothian Rd, West End ☎ 0871/224 4007, ⊛ www.odeon.co.uk. Central four-screen cinema showing the latest releases.

Ster Century Ocean Terminal, Ocean Drive, Leith ☎ 0131/553 0700, ⊛ www .stercentury.co.uk. Buses #1, #11, #22, #34, #35. Big multiplex in the developing docklands, with plenty of bars and restaurants nearby.

UGC Fountainpark Dundee St, Fountainbridge ☎ 0871/200 2000, ⊛ www .ugccinemas.co.uk. Buses #1, #28, #34 & #35. Big, reasonably central multiplex not far from Tollcross and Brunsfield.

Warner Village Omni Centre Greenside Place, Broughton ☎ 0871/224 0240, ⊛ www.warnervillage.co.uk. Most central of Edinburgh's big multi-screen venues, tucked under Calton Hill at the top of Leith Walk.

The Edinburgh Festival

For the best part of August, the character of Scotland's capital is completely transformed by the **Edinburgh Festival**, the world's largest celebration of the arts. Every available performance space – from the grandest concert halls to pub courtyards – plays host to a packed programme of cultural entertainment, ranging from world-class opera to student revues. The streets fill with buskers and craft stalls, and the local population swells to twice its normal size as tourists, performers, media types and festival-goers throng the city centre. Pubs and restaurants stay open later, and the atmosphere in town takes on a surreal but energized buzz.

The Edinburgh Festival is actually an umbrella term which encompasses different festivals taking place at around

the same time in the city. The principal events are the Edinburgh International Festival and the much larger Edinburgh Festival Fringe, but there are also Film, Book, Jazz and Blues and Television festivals, the Military Tattoo on the Castle Esplanade and the Edinburgh Mela, an Asian festival held over a weekend in late August/early September.

The Edinburgh International Festival

The **Edinburgh International Festival** (sometimes called the "Official Festival") was the original Edinburgh Festival, conceived in 1947 as a celebration of pan-European culture in the post-war era. Initially dominated by opera, other

Doing the Festival

For the visitor, the sheer volume of the Festival's output can be bewildering: virtually every branch of arts and entertainment is represented somewhere, and world-famous stars mix with pub singers in the daily line-up. It can be a struggle to find accommodation, get hold of the tickets you want, book a table in a restaurant or simply get from one side of town to another; you can end up seeing something truly dire, or something mind-blowing; you'll inevitably try to do too much, stay out too late or spend too much money – but then again, most Festival veterans will tell you that if you don't experience these things then you haven't really done the Festival.

Dates, venues, names, star acts, happening bars and burning issues change from one year to the next. This unpredictability is one of the Festival's greatest charms, however, so while the following information will help you get to grips with it, be prepared for – indeed, enjoy – the unexpected. For up-to-the-minute information at any time of year, visit ⌘ www.edinburghfestivals.co.uk, which has links to the home pages of most of the main festivals. Each festival produces its own programme well in advance, while during the Festival various publications give information about what's on day-by-day, among them *The Guide*, published daily by the Fringe Office, and local what's-on guide *The List*, which comes out weekly during the Festival and manages to combine comprehensive coverage with a reliably on-the-pulse sense of what's hot and what's not. Of the local newspapers, *The Scotsman* carries a dedicated daily Festival supplement with an events diary and reviews which carry a lot of weight, while *The Herald*, published in Glasgow, and the London-based papers offer more selective but generally authoritative reviews. Various freebie newspapers are also available around town – best of these is *Fest*, which mixes news with pithy reviews and yet more listings.

▼ Ghost tours

Let costumed characters lead you on spine-tingling visits to the graveyards and haunted corners of Edinburgh's underworld.

P.69 ▶ THE ROYAL MILE

▼ Greyfriars Bobby statue

Edinburgh's most sentimental statue, honouring the loyal terrier who watched over his master's grave for fourteen years.

P.93 ▶ SOUTH OF THE ROYAL MILE

▲ Calton Old Burial Ground

A wealth of intriguing gravestones and memorials to citizens both famous and obscure.

P.119 ▶ CALTON HILL AND BROUGHTON

▲ The Last Drop Tavern

This convivial pub pays tribute to the public hangings which once took place across the road.

P.101 ▶ SOUTH OF THE ROYAL MILE

Literary Edinburgh

Edinburgh status as UNESCO's first World City of Literature is testament to the writers, poets and publishers who have moulded its prominent literary culture. Lions such as Sir Walter Scott and Robert Louis Stevenson enjoy numerous memorials and references around Edinburgh, while literary tours allow you to follow up local links with many other characters and authors, from Sherlock Holmes and Harry Potter to Irvine Welsh and Ian Rankin.

▼ Literary pub tour

A convivial jaunt in words and whisky around the pubs frequented by the city's famous writers.

P.69 ▶ THE ROYAL MILE

▼ Scott Monument

This huge Gothic rocket on Princes Street commemorates Sir Walter Scott, author of *Ivanhoe* and the Waverley novels.

P.106 ▶ ALONG PRINCES STREET

▲ McNaughtan's bookshop

The best of the city's secondhand book-shops, stacked high with well-thumbed novels and pristine first editions.

P.124 ▸ CALTON HILL AND BROUGHTON

▲ Oxford Bar

Still unspoiled, this is the preferred drinking spot of both Inspector Rebus and his creator, Ian Rankin.

P.118 ▸ THE NEW TOWN

▼ Writers' museum

Reams of memorabilia relating to Edin-burgh's greatest literary giants: Walter Scott, Robert Louis Stevenson and Robert Burns.

P.72 ▸ THE ROYAL MILE

▼ Elephant House

One of the Old Town cafés where J.K. Rowl-ing sought a warm corner to scribble the first Harry Potter story.

P.98 ▸ SOUTH OF THE ROYAL MILE

Galleries and museums

In its art galleries and museums, Edinburgh has all the wealth and privilege of a capital city, with Scotland's finest art and artefacts presented in a series of impressive buildings. The national collections here are not daunting in size, with most relatively easy to digest in an hour or two's viewing, and entry to almost all is free. Venture beyond them, and you'll also find a rich, varied range of private and commercial galleries showcasing vibrant contemporary talent.

▲ Royal Museum of Scotland

The airy iron-framed nineteenth-century interior houses a wealth of antiquities from around the world.

P.94 ▶ SOUTH OF THE ROYAL MILE

▲ Fruitmarket Gallery

The city's most dynamic exhibition space, devoted to changing exhibitions of international twenty-first century art.

P.104 ▶ ALONG PRINCES STREET

▼ National Gallery of Scotland

The intimate rooms here display works by Botticelli, Titian, Rembrandt, the Impressionists and Scotland's finest pre-twentieth-century artists.

P.106 ▶ ALONG PRINCES STREET

▲ Dean Gallery

Taking up two whole storeys, Paolozzi's massive *Vulcan* is the highlight of this superb collection of modern art.

P.130 ▶ ALONG THE WATER OF LEITH

▼ Dundas Street galleries

An inspiring series of private and commercial galleries, many specializing in local contemporary artists.

P.113 ▶ THE NEW TOWN

▲ National Museum of Scotland

This imaginatively designed modern building holds Scotland's premier collection of historic artefacts.

P.93 ▶ SOUTH OF THE ROYAL MILE

Sports and activities

Edinburgh's contribution to the history of sport is unexpectedly significant: the rules of golf were drawn up in Leith, while the world's first ever rugby international was played on a local cricket ground. Today, rugby internationals at Murrayfield are colourful, passionate events; if participation is more your thing, head for the world's largest indoor climbing arena, or take to Edinburgh's many green spaces, which are perfect for jogging, cycling, walking or even flying a kite.

▼ Arthur's Seat

The open green spaces of Holyrood Park offer walkers an inviting taste of the rugged Scottish Highlands.

P.88 ▸ HOLYROOD AND ARTHUR'S SEAT

▼ Loony Dook

The traditional South Queensferry way to welcome the New Year is a swim in the Firth of Forth. It's not compulsory, but it is cold.

P.152 ▸ SOUTH QUEENSFERRY AND THE FORTH BRIDGES

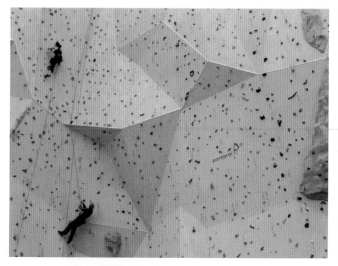

▲ Ratho Adventure Centre

Some of the world's finest indoor climbing facilities can be found at this remarkable new complex.

P.143 ▸ NORTH AND WEST EDINBURGH

▼ Rugby

Played in front of noisy crowds of 65,000, Scotland's home international fixtures are usually stirring encounters.

P.141 ▸ NORTH AND WEST EDINBURGH

▲ Golf

Edinburgh has numerous excellent courses, including a number of public and short-hole courses.

P.182 ▸ ESSENTIALS

Traditional pubs

It's often said that if the weather in Scotland was any better, the pubs wouldn't be so good. Edinburgh has more than its fair share of classic venues, from low-beamed rooms tucked into Old Town basements to splendid Victorian bars graced with ornate cornicing and magnificent tiled walls. And it's not just whisky that flows freely – Edinburgh also has a long tradition as a centre of beer-brewing.

▲ Bow Bar

An unaffected champion of Edinburgh's old-style bars, with a lip-smacking range of real ales and single malt whiskies.

P.101 ▸ SOUTH OF THE ROYAL MILE

▲ Café Royal Circle Bar

A magnificent listed interior featuring mahogany carvings and hand-painted tiles, as well as good food and beer on tap.

P.109 ▸ ALONG PRINCES STREET

▼ Cumberland Bar

A discerning choice for a beer and good conversation in the New Town

P.118 ▸ THE NEW TOWN

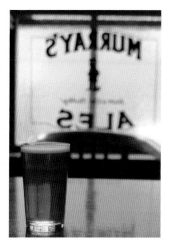

▼ Sheep Heid Inn

The highlight of the urban village of Duddingston is this local pub and its old-fashioned skittle alley.

P.89 ▸ HOLYROOD AND ARTHUR'S SEAT

▲ The Shore

This wood- and mirror-lined haunt abuts the water in Leith's old harbour.

P.138 ▸ LEITH

▲ Jolly Judge

A tiny pub tucked away in a hidden courtyard just off the oldest part of Royal Mile.

P.81 ▸ THE ROYAL MILE

Classical Edinburgh

Planned and built in the eighteenth century, Edinburgh's elegant New Town offered a unique opportunity for Classically-influenced architects of the time to bring grandeur and magnificence to the cityscape. Edinburgh was soon dubbed the "Athens of the North", and construction of a mock-Parthenon on Calton Hill began; this half-completed monument may still be known as "Edinburgh's Disgrace", but the Classical legacy elsewhere in the city is quite the opposite.

▼ Hopetoun House

Scotland's grandest stately home is a magnificent tribute to the Neoclassical vision of the Adam family of architects.

P.153 ▶ SOUTH QUEENSFERRY AND THE FORTH BRIDGES

▼ Calton Hill

The strange collection of nineteenth-century buildings and memorials here include the unfinished National Monument.

P.119 ▶ CALTON HILL AND BROUGHTON

▲ St Bernard's Well

This elegant Doric rotunda adds an Arcadian aspect to the Water of Leith.

P.126 ▸ ALONG THE WATER OF LEITH

▲ National Gallery of Scotland

One of two Grecian temples built right in the heart of the capital to house Scotland's collection of art treasures.

P.106 ▸ ALONG PRINCES STREET

▼ Georgian House

A National Trust for Scotland property furnished to show off the grandeur of early nineteenth century living.

P.113 ▸ THE NEW TOWN

▼ New Town

One of Europe's finest residential quarters, with rows and terraces of dignified Georgian architecture.

P.110 ▸ THE NEW TOWN

Restaurants and cafés

Edinburgh's restaurant scene offers an alluring combination of culinary flair, dramatic design and sumptuous preparation. The local seafood, beef and venison is among the best available, and has been imaginatively utilized by chefs to create a unique style of modern Scottish cuisine. Hand-in-hand with this new confidence has come a café culture worthy of any vibrant European capital – you may not always be able to drink it al fresco, but a frothy cappuccino in a classy café isn't hard to find.

▲ David Bann's
One of Edinburgh's hippest places to eat, with a varied and interesting meat-free menu.

P.79 ▸ THE ROYAL MILE

▲ Fishers
One of Leith's best-renowned seafood bistros, offering appealing, daily changing menus based around fresh Scottish fish.

P.137 ▸ LEITH

▼ The Tower

With its memorable setting high up in the National Museum of Scotland, this is one of Edinburgh's most impressive upmarket restaurants.

P.100 ▸ SOUTH OF THE ROYAL MILE

▲ Fruitmarket Gallery Café

The Fruitmarket gallery's excellent café is a great spot for a coffee or light lunch right in the city centre.

P.108 ▸ ALONG PRINCES STREET

▼ The Grain Store

An understated interior and an impressive Scottish menu make this a great place for a casual but sophisticated meal.

P.99 ▸ SOUTH OF THE ROYAL MILE

▲ Glass & Thompson

A classy sandwich or fresh pastry here is an essential part of any New Town exploration.

P.116 ▸ THE NEW TOWN

Secret Edinburgh

Edinburgh is so full of important buildings and grand architecture that in the procession from one to the other it's easy to overlook the city's less obvious draws. Yet there are many hidden corners – not just in the Old Town, where there seem to be secrets down every close and even under the ground, but also out from the centre, where ancient villages hold onto their identity despite having been subsumed into the capital.

▼ Vaults tour

Take a tour of the town below the ground to discover the city's catacombs, vaults and subterranean passageways.

P.69 ▸ THE ROYAL MILE

▲ Dean Village

This charming, secluded little community of converted mill buildings is one of the landmarks on the Water of Leith Walkway.

P.128 ▸ ALONG THE WATER OF LEITH

▲ The Witchery by The Castle

The gothic-themed Secret Garden room here was decorated by white witches, and top chefs work their magic in the kitchen.

P.80 ▸ THE ROYAL MILE

▼ Dunbar's Close Garden

Tucked down a Royal Mile close, this tiny formal garden is an inspiring and tranquil retreat from the bustling city centre.

P.76 ▸ THE ROYAL MILE

▼ Mary King's Close

Edinburgh's "lost city" is a remarkably well preserved series of Old Town houses and closes in the basement of the City Chambers.

P.74 ▸ THE ROYAL MILE

Gourmet Edinburgh

Edinburgh has a long history when it comes to a taste for the good things in life. The revered Valvona & Crolla deli opened here in 1934, while whisky merchants such as William Cadenhead have been around since the nineteenth century. Both remain star attractions of the city's impressive range of gourmet experiences, specialist food shops and delicatessens, which also includes a regular farmers' market, showcasing produce from in and around the city.

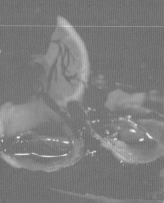

▲ Valvona & Crolla

Possibly the finest Italian deli in Britain, this is a truly inspiring emporium of the finest fresh foods, fine wines and epicurean treats.

P.124 ▸ CALTON HILL AND BROUGHTON

▼ Oysters

Fresh from the west coast of Scotland, local oysters are a staple of Edinburgh's seafood bistros and restaurants.

P.109 ▶ ALONG PRINCES STREET

▲ Farmers' market

Top-quality meat, fish, cheese, bread and vegetables sold in the shadow of the castle.

P.97 ▶ SOUTH OF THE ROYAL MILE

▼ Cadenhead's

This small, unassuming shop sells a bewildering range of whiskies, including many rare and specially bottled distillations.

P.77 ▶ THE ROYAL MILE

▲ Iain Mellis Cheesemonger

With three shops piled high with rounds of delicious British and continental cheeses, Mr Mellis is well worth sniffing out.

P.97 ▶ SOUTH OF THE ROYAL MILE

Clubs and style bars

Edinburgh's vibrant nightlife scene covers all the genres, from dub to disco and chillout to comedy, but the most memorable aspect of a night out here is the range and variety of venues. The "style bars" try to outdo their competitors with up-to-the-minute design, while others make the most of ornate former banks and offices, and clubs occupy ever more unusual locations, with nights staged in old churches, smart Georgian mansions and even the Royal Mile's vaults.

▼ The Dome

This stunning cocktail bar and restaurant in a converted bank is a sophisticated spot for a drink or meal.

P.118 ▶ THE NEW TOWN

▼ Honeycomb

The Old Town's catacombs provide a unique venue for some of the city's top DJs.

P.173 ▶ ESSENTIALS

▲ Fishtank

A great little New Town bar for those into mellow grooves and goldfish.

P.118 ▸ THE NEW TOWN

▼ Human Be-In

Hip hangout for students and Southsiders, with foreign lagers, classic contemporary decor and an enlightened food menu.

P.150 ▸ SOUTH EDINBURGH

▼ Opal Lounge

The flashiest place to be seen (if not heard) on Edinburgh's glitz strip, George Street.

P.118 ▸ THE NEW TOWN

▲ Stand Comedy Club

Edinburgh's top venue for stand-up keeps the giggles going seven days a week, twelve months a year.

P.175 ▸ ESSENTIALS

Gay Edinburgh

For all Edinburgh's reputation as a dour, stern, Calvinist city, the gay quarter here is well-established in bohemian Broughton on the edge of the New Town. In addition to a number of gay cafés, bars and nightclubs, most of them straight-friendly and a familiar part of the social circuit, there are stylish gay-run guesthouses and colourful annual events celebrating the gay community in Scotland.

▲ **Pride Scotia festival**

Annual parade and celebration held on alternate years in Edinburgh and Glasgow.

P.180 ▸ ESSENTIALS

▼ Ardmor House

This gay-owned guesthouse ranks among the most contemporary and stylish small places to stay in Edinburgh.

P.165 ▶ ACCOMMODATION

▲ CC Blooms

Edinburgh's sole uniquely gay nightclub is always loud, lively and popular.

P.174 ▶ ESSENTIALS

▼ Blue Moon Café

The city's longest-established and best-known gay café, right in the heart of things off Broughton Street.

P.124 ▶ CALTON HILL AND
BROUGHTON

▲ Planet Out

One of the main meeting points of Edinburgh's gay scene, this drinking spot rocks as a busy pre-club bar.

P.125 ▶ CALTON HILL AND
BROUGHTON

Indulgent Edinburgh

If you're after a treat during your visit to Edinburgh, you'll find an increasing number of places which open the door to a bit of lavishness. Indulge in a cup of the world's best hot chocolate or dine from the kitchen of a Michelin-starred chef; float away from your troubles at a top-ranked spa; or take advantage of one of Edinburgh's luxury places to stay, which include a romantic castle and an OTT Gothic apartment in the heart of the Old Town.

▼ Plaisir du Chocolat

This chocolatier and refined Parisian-style café is worth visiting for its range of exquisite hot chocolate drinks alone.

P.78 ▶ THE ROYAL MILE

▲ Restaurant Martin Wishart

Intricate French culinary techniques brought to bear on top-notch Scottish produce.

P.137 ▶ LEITH

▼ Witchery apartments

These unique themed rooms are a riot of indulgent baroque decor and escapist pampering.

P.161 ▶ ACCOMMODATION

▼ Dalhousie Castle

A 700-year old castle on the outskirts of Edinburgh, beautifully converted into a luxurious country house hotel and spa.

P.167 ▶ ACCOMMODATION

▲ One Spa, Sheraton Grand

This superb ultra-modern hotel spa includes a range of revitalizing treatments, including a hydropool on the roof.

P.164 ▶ ACCOMMODATION

Festivals and events

Edinburgh likes to dub itself the "Festival City", but that doesn't just apply to August – at almost any time of year you'll find colourful events and celebrations which take in subjects as diverse as the locally brewed ales and hairy highland cattle. Some of these events link back to pagan ritual and are still celebrated with gusto – none more so than at the massive city-centre street party which marks Hogmanay, as New Year's Eve is known to Scots.

▲ Hogmanay

Edinburgh's massive New Year's Eve street party involves live bands, dancing, fireworks and 100,000 people singing *Auld Lang Syne*.

P.181 ▸ ESSENTIALS

▼ Capital Christmas

Edinburgh's winter festival sees an outdoor skating rink installed in Princes Street Gardens.

P.181 › ESSENTIALS

▲ Beltane Fire Festival

Ancient Celtic celebrations marking the arrival of spring are re-created in a colourful night-time pageant on Calton Hill.

P.180 › ESSENTIALS

▼ Caledonian Beer Festival

The city's traditionally brewed beers line up alongside the best of Britain's real ales in this annual two-day celebration.

P.180 › ESSENTIALS

▲ Royal Highland Show

Scotland's premier agricultural show is a big deal for farmers and townies alike – and well worth getting dressed up for.

P.180 › ESSENTIALS

Green places

48

Edinburgh's civic parks and protected green spaces are unique and incredibly varied. Central Edinburgh boasts rows of blossom-heavy trees and a beautifully manicured garden reclaimed from a stagnant loch, and there's also a lush 800-foot high peak within a mile of the centre, once part of the king's hunting ground. And if you feel like getting active, there are plenty of open spaces geared up for cycling, football or just sitting around.

▼ Calton Hill

This distinctive landmark combines tall trees, grassy banks and wild gorse bushes as well as some off-beat architecture.

←P.119 ▸ CALTON HILL AND BROUGHTON

▼ Royal Botanic Garden

These seventy beautifully tended acres are perfect for lazy strolls.

P.126 ▸ ALONG THE WATER OF LEITH

▲ Water of Leith

This verdant escape from the city centre links up a number of the sights worth seeing to the north of Edinburgh.

P.126 ▶ ALONG THE WATER OF LEITH

▲ Holyrood Park

This spectacular sweep of heathery moor and craggy cliff includes precipitous Arthur's Seat.

P.87 ▶ HOLYROOD AND ARTHUR'S SEAT

▼ Princes Street Gardens

This wide swathe of lawn and mature trees makes a beautiful division between the Old and New towns.

P.105 ▶ ALONG PRINCES STREET

▼ The Meadows

With its cycle paths and sports fields, the Meadows are perfect for getting active.

P.145 ▶ SOUTH EDINBURGH

Edinburgh views

Few European capitals offer so many different and dramatic vistas as hilly Edinburgh. It's a breathtaking city to explore on foot, with every steep climb rewarded with panoramic overviews across the rooftops to city landmarks, distant peaks and the shimmering Firth of Forth. And it's not just the topography that delivers – there are towers, bridges and even restaurants where you've little option but to stand (or sit) and stare.

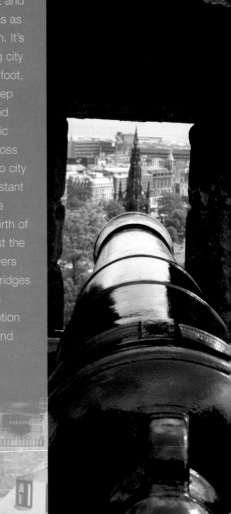

▲ Edinburgh Castle

From the castle's ancient ramparts you can enjoy a 360-degree outlook on the city – and any nearby invading armies.

P.67 ▸ THE ROYAL MILE

▼ Calton Hill

Whenever there's sunshine on Leith, you'll see it best from Calton Hill.

P.119 ▸ CALTON HILL AND BROUGHTON

▲ Salisbury Crags

The Radical Road footpath here offers a subtly changing overview of Holyrood and the new Parliament building.

P.87 ▸ HOLYROOD AND ARTHUR'S SEAT

▼ Royal Botanic Garden

The panoramic views from the Botanics are dominated by the jagged Old Town skyline.

P.126 ▸ ALONG THE WATER OF LEITH

▲ Oloroso

In good weather, the terrace of this swanky restaurant is *the* place to head for stunning scenic views over the chimneypots.

P.117 ▸ THE NEW TOWN

Kids' Edinburgh

With spiral staircases and battlements to explore, "haunted" ruins full of beguiling nooks and crannies and lots of open spaces in which to just charge around, Edinburgh has plenty to amuse young visitors. And while many of the major historic sites will undoubtedly appeal to kids' imagination, there are also a number of excellent attractions specifically targeted at children – welcome respite if the city's emphasis on walking has worn out those younger legs.

▼ Ratho Adventure Centre

This exciting new climbing centre has impressive facilities for kids, including an exhilarating aerial assault course.

P.143 ▶ NORTH AND WEST EDINBURGH

▲ Brass Rubbing Centre

Discover the timeless delights of brass rubbing in a converted church just off the Royal Mile.

P.74 ▸ THE ROYAL MILE

▼ Scottish Mining Museum

An unusual heritage museum in a converted colliery, where the tour includes a trip underground to the old coalface.

P.149 ▸ SOUTH EDINBURGH

▼ Edinburgh Zoo

Various breeds of all-action penguin are among the star attractions at the city's excellent zoo.

P.139 ▸ NORTH AND WEST EDINBURGH

▲ Our Dynamic Earth

Edinburgh's science centre uses a bit of hi-tech "time travel" to introduce the wonders of the natural world.

P.86 ▸ HOLYROOD AND ARTHUR'S SEAT

Modern architecture

For somewhere so famous for its rich history, much of it bound up in medieval buildings and Classical architecture, it's easy to overlook the dynamism of Edinburgh's contemporary buildings. Led by the eyecatching new parliament, innovative design is suddenly very much part of the Edinburgh picture, and there's a new-found appreciation of the contributions of modern architecture, both residential and in public buildings, to the already dramatic cityscape.

Hawthornden Stair

▲ National Museum of Scotland

The custom-built museum is fascinating in itself, with labyrinthine corridors, oddly shaped rooms and occasional shafts of light and space.

P.93 ▶ SOUTH OF THE ROYAL MILE

▼ Fishmarket Close

These new apartments in the heart of the Old Town are a highly successful modern interpretation of the area's traditional medieval tenements.

P.67 ▸ THE ROYAL MILE

▲ Point Hotel

This converted department store is one of Edinburgh's most stylish places to stay, with interior decor at the cutting edge of contemporary design.

P.164 ▸ SOUTH OF THE ROYAL MILE

▼ Dance Base

A brilliant example of how a modern structure, full of light and clever angles, can be fitted into a typically constricted Old Town space.

P.92 ▸ SOUTH OF THE ROYAL MILE

▲ Scottish Parliament

Enric Miralles' troubled yet thrilling design is a memorable tribute to his quirky approach, attention to detail and love of stylized imagery.

P.84 ▸ HOLYROOD AND ARTHUR'S SEAT

Eccentric Edinburgh

Enfolded within Edinburgh's layers of history are many peculiar stories and eccentricities. This is a very individual capital, a unique assembly of geography, architecture, creativity and ambition, so it's perhaps no great surprise that such a mix has manifested in some delightful flights of fancy. And as you explore, you'll find that the discovery of Edinburgh's odder buildings and its less-than-conventional side can undoubtedly lighten the serious side of sightseeing.

▼ Prestonfield

This wonderfully extravagant hotel is a sumptuous, baroque fantasy, filled with brocade drapes, velvet cushions, antique furniture and exquisite cornicing.

P.167 ▸ ACCOMMODATION

▼ Scottish National Portrait Gallery

Not content with a cityscape dotted with Greek temples, Edinburgh also has its own version of the Venetian Doge's Palace

P.110 ▸ THE NEW TOWN

▲ Rosslyn Chapel

The intricate carvings of Biblical images, secretive symbols and hidden messages here are seen by some as evidence of an intricate historical-religious conspiracy.

P.148 ▸ SOUTH EDINBURGH

▼ Surgeon's Hall Museum

The rows and rows of jars containing body parts, preserved organs and diseased specimens here are gruesome but quite compelling.

P.96 ▸ SOUTH OF THE ROYAL MILE

▼ National Monument

This rather incongruous half-completed replica of Athens' Parthenon adds a hint of grandeur to the city's skyline.

P.121 ▸ CALTON HILL AND BROUGHTON

Shopping

Although the shops on Edinburgh's famous Princes Street can be a bit of a disappointment, you only have to shift a block away to George Street to find glamorous boutiques and upmarket emporia. Elsewhere in the city, it's often the smaller traders on the backstreets which capture the imagination: look out in particular for knitwear designers, antiquarian booksellers, jewellers and arts and crafts galleries.

▲ Jenners

The grande dame of Edinburgh shops, this old-fashioned department store has overseen the comings and goings of Princes Street for more than a century.

P.108 ▶ ALONG PRINCES STREET

▲ Corniche

This small but perfectly formed boutique sells interesting ladies' and men's designerwear straight from the catwalks.

P.77 ▶ THE ROYAL MILE

▼ Victoria Street

The city's quaintest shopping street, with a string of unusual one-off shops that include a portmanteau maker and a cheesemonger.

P.97 ▶ SOUTH OF THE ROYAL MILE

▼ Harvey Nichols

The chic new kid on Edinburgh's shopping block, with four floors of all the most important designer labels.

P.115 ▶ THE NEW TOWN

▲ St Stephen Street

This intriguing Stockbridge sidestreet has a low-key collection of pubs, places to eat, secondhand clothes boutiques and craft shops.

P.127 ▶ ALONG THE WATER OF LEITH

▲ Anta

An appealing contemporary approach to tartans and tweed, specializing in bags, scarves, throws and fabrics.

P.97 ▶ SOUTH OF THE ROYAL MILE

Nautical Edinburgh

Edinburgh's former port, Leith retains an independent spirit born of cosmopolitan trade and seafaring connections as well as the need to reinvent now that shipping has changed entirely – the most prominent vessel docked here today is the former Royal yacht *Britannia*, now a major tourist attraction. Edinburgh's other seaside suburbs – Cramond and South Queensferry – offer an equally salty air, and you can even catch a glimpse of the sea right in the centre from Calton Hill's signal mast.

▼ Cramond

The River Almond meets the Firth of Forth at Cramond, a charming spot for a bracing seaside promenade.

P.142 ▶ NORTH AND WEST EDINBURGH

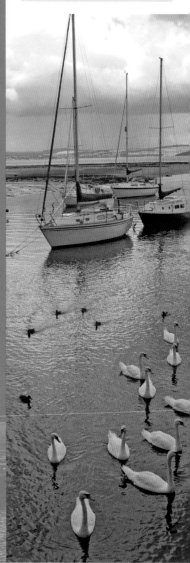

▲ Nelson Monument

This oddly-shaped monument to England's most famous sailor is topped with an elevated viewing platform looking across Edinburgh and out to sea.

P.121 ▸ CALTON HILL AND
BROUGHTON

▲ The Shore

Symbols of seafaring days abound along Leith's old harbour, now lined with pleasant pubs and places to eat.

P.134 ▸ LEITH

▼ South Queensferry

This historic town perched on the shore of the Firth of Forth is the best place to take in the mighty Forth Bridges.

P.151 ▸ SOUTH QUEENSFERRY AND
THE FORTH BRIDGES

▼ Royal Yacht Britannia

Climb aboard to check that everything's as ship-shape as it was when *Britannia* was touring the world with the Royal family.

P.135 ▸ LEITH

Art outdoors

Edinburgh has a flourishing artistic tradition which is, inevitably, mostly celebrated indoors in the city's numerous art galleries. However, sculptors are among the artists most cherished by the city, and the compelling works of contemporary public art that are dotted all over the capital provide a quirky, unexpected antidote to the grand (if rather serious) architecture and impressive vistas which inevitably surround them.

▲ Cone

Andy Goldsworthy's slate pine cone is one of a number of artworks dotted around Edinburgh's Botanic Garden.

P.126 ▸ ALONG THE WATER OF LEITH

▼ Sculpture trail

The outdoor sculpture trail which leads through the grounds of the Scottish National Gallery of Modern Art and the neighbouring Dean Gallery includes works by Moore, Hepworth and Whiteread.

P.129 ▶ ALONG THE WATER OF LEITH

▲ Pigeon sculptures

Shona Kinloch's bronze birdies scratch around on the pavement at Elm Row, near the top of Leith Walk.

P.119 ▶ CALTON HILL AND BROUGHTON

▼ Landform

Charles Jenks' sinuous series of ponds and grassy mounds dominate the grounds of the Scottish National Gallery of Modern Art.

P.129 ▶ ALONG THE WATER OF LEITH

▲ Manuscript of Monte Cassino

Check out the distinctive pop art of local hero Eduardo Paolozzi in a pedestrian precinct near the top of Broughton Street.

P.122 ▶ CALTON HILL AND BROUGHTON

Places

The Royal Mile

With its historic old buildings, closely packed tenements and shadowy closes, the Royal Mile ranks as one of the great streets of the world. Running downhill along a ridge from the cliff-skirted castle above the city to the Palace of Holyroodhouse, the Royal Mile remains medieval in character (if not always in reality), and is still the most resonant part of the Old Town, with a palpable sense that over the centuries most of Scottish history has passed this way. Even today it's at the heart of Scottish affairs, with politicians, judges and journalists mixing with the throngs of tourists ambling between the sights and souvenir shops.

Edinburgh Castle

Castlehill ☎0131/225 9846, ⊛www .historic-scotland.gov.uk. Daily: April–Oct 9.30am–6pm; Nov–March 9.30am–5pm. £9.50. Even given the wealth of Edinburgh's grand and historic sights, it's still the castle that defines the city. Perched on its high, impregnable crag of volcanic rock and protected by sheer cliffs on three sides, it has played a vital strategic role in Scottish affairs for hundreds of years. It was here that Mary, Queen of Scots, gave birth to her only child, James IV (the final king to use the citadel as a royal palace), and it last saw action in 1745, when

Bonnie Prince Charlie's forces made a half-hearted attempt to storm it. The disparate styles of the fortifications reflect the change in its role from defensive citadel to national monument, and today, as well as attracting more visitors than anywhere else in the country, the castle is still

▼MILLS MOUNT BATTERY, EDINBURGH CASTLE

What's in a mile

The Royal Mile is, in fact, one mile 110 yards in length, measuring from the castle drawbridge to the gates of Holyroodhouse. It has different names at various points along its length: the short, narrow section from the castle to the roundabout outside The Hub is called Castlehill. At this point it becomes the Lawnmarket; while east of the main junction with the Mound and George IV Bridge it is the High Street. The final section, after the junction with St Mary's Street, is the Canongate.

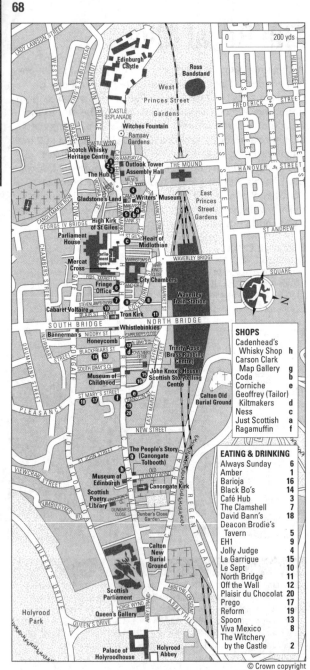

Edinburgh Castle

Ross Bandstand

West Princes Street Gardens

Witches Fountain

Ramsay Gardens

Scotch Whisky Heritage Centre

Outlook Tower
Assembly Hall

The Hub

Gladstone's Land

Writers' Museum

East Princes Street Gardens

High Kirk of St Giles

Parliament House

Heart of Midlothian

Mercat Cross

City Chambers

Fringe Office

Waverley Train Station

Cabaret Voltaire

Tron Kirk

Whistlebinkies

Bannerman's

Honeycomb

Trinity Apse (Brass Rubbing Centre)

Museum of Childhood

John Knox's House/ Scottish Storytelling Centre

Calton Old Burial Ground

The People's Story (Canongate Tolbooth)

Museum of Edinburgh

Canongate Kirk

Scottish Poetry Library

Dunbar's Close Garden

Calton New Burial Ground

Scottish Parliament

Queen's Gallery

Holyrood Park

Palace of Holyroodhouse

Holyrood Abbey

0   200 yds

SHOPS

Cadenhead's Whisky Shop	h
Carson Clark Map Gallery	g
Coda	b
Corniche	e
Geoffrey (Tailor) Kiltmakers	d
Ness	c
Just Scottish	a
Ragamuffin	f

EATING & DRINKING

Always Sunday	6
Amber	1
Barioja	16
Black Bo's	14
Café Hub	3
The Clamshell	7
David Bann's	18
Deacon Brodie's Tavern	5
EH1	9
Jolly Judge	4
La Garrigue	15
Le Sept	10
North Bridge	11
Off the Wall	12
Plaisir du Chocolat	20
Prego	17
Reform	19
Spoon	13
Viva Mexico	8
The Witchery by the Castle	2

Tours on (and under) the Royal Mile

It isn't hard to get a sense of history by strolling down the Royal Mile on your own, but if you really want to load up on facts and colourful anecdotes, sign up with one of the companies that offer guided historic walking tours here, including Mercat (☎0131/557 6464, ⊛www.mercat-tours.co.uk) and Auld Reekie (☎0131/557 4700, ⊛www.auldreekietours.co.uk). Both companies also offer a chance to explore the vaults and subterranean streets immediately under the Royal Mile; dark deeds and spooky stories abound on these expeditions, as they do on more explicit ghost tours conducted by the ghoulishly-dressed actors of the Witchery Tour (☎0131/225 6745, ⊛www.witcherytours.com) and City of the Dead Tours (☎0131/225 9044, ⊛www.blackhart.uk.com), who take groups on spine-tingling night-time graveyard visits. If you prefer your imagination to be roused in other ways, the Edinburgh Literary Pub Tour (☎0131/226 6665, ⊛www.edinburghliterarypubtour.co.uk) mixes a convivial pub crawl with extracts from local authors acted out along the way.

The above tours cost in the region of £7–8 and most leave from the area opposite or outside the City Chambers, where the various companies have signboards set up.

▲ROYAL MILE WALKING TOURS

a working military garrison as well as home to Scotland's crown jewels.

Though entry is quite pricey, there's plenty to take in, from dingy prisons to windy battlements. At the heart of the complex is Crown Square, where you'll find the Great Hall and the quietly reverential Scottish National War Memorial, as well as the Crown Room, where the nation's magnificent crown jewels are displayed beside the Stone of Destiny, a plain lump of masonry on which all kings of Scotland since Kenneth MacAlpine in 893 have been crowned.

Elsewhere you'll find the interesting but not overly militaristic National War Museum of Scotland, smaller regimental museums and St Margaret's Chapel, the oldest surviving building in Edinburgh, constructed in the twelfth century by King David I as a memorial to his mother. The battlements in front of the chapel offer the best of all the castle's panoramic views, as well as a chance to look down the barrel of the fifteenth-century siege gun Mons Meg, which could launch a 500-pound cannonball nearly two miles. The castle's other famous cannon is the more modern piece of artillery which fires a single daily round (Mon–Sat) from Mills Mount Battery at one o'clock. Originally designed for the benefit of ships in the Firth of Forth, the firing now provides a popular ceremony for visitors and a ritualized time signal for city-centre office workers.

Castle Esplanade

If you don't have the time or inclination to visit the castle itself, the Esplanade leading up to its drawbridge offers a taste of the precipitous location and eye-stretching views. Originally

▲RAMSAY GARDENS APARTMENTS

a parade ground, it serves as a coach park for much of the year these days, with huge temporary grandstands taking over in July and August for the Edinburgh Military Tattoo (see p.179), a shameless if spectacular pageant of swinging kilts and massed pipe bands. At the northeast corner of the esplanade, near the fairytale turrets and odd angles of the Ramsay Gardens apartments, look out for the Witches' Fountain, an Art Nouveau plaque commemorating some three hundred women burned near the spot on charges of sorcery, the last of whom was put to death in 1722.

Scotch Whisky Heritage Centre

354 Castlehill ☏ 0131/220 0441, ⊛ www.whisky-heritage.co.uk. Daily: Oct–April 10am–6pm; May–Sept 9.30am–6.30pm. £7.95. This city-centre showcase for Scotland's national drink mimics the kind of tours offered at distilleries in the Highlands and Islands, and while it can't match the authenticity of the real thing, the centre does offer a thorough introduction to the "water of life" (*uisge beatha* in Gaelic). Tours start off with a dram (measure) of whisky, then move through a scale model of a distillery and an entertaining tutorial on the specialized art of blending, and conclude with a gimmicky ride in a moving "barrel" car through a series of uninspiring historical tableaux. On the ground floor, a well-stocked shop gives an idea of the sheer range and diversity of the drink, while downstairs there's a pleasant whisky bar and restaurant (see p.79).

Outlook Tower

Castlehill ☏ 0131/226 3709, ⊛ www.camera-obscura.co.uk. Daily: April–Oct 9.30am–6pm; July–Aug 9.30am–7.30pm; Nov–March 9am–5pm. £6.25. Housed in the domed black-and-white turret atop the Outlook Tower, Edinburgh's camera obscura has been a tourist attraction since 1853, providing an intriguing bird's-eye view of a city going about its business. The "camera" consists of a small darkened room with a white wooden table onto which a periscope reflects live images of prominent buildings and folk walking on the streets below. In a world of webcams and hi-tech imagery, the camera obscura retains an appealing simplicity and nostalgic charm, though the

World of Illusions exhibition which occupies the other floors of the tower (included in the ticket price) does have a much more futuristic theme, displaying colourful holograms, 3-D pictures and other optical games with an obvious appeal to children.

The Hub

Castlehill ☎0131/473 2010, ⊛www .eif.co.uk/thehub. Ticket office Mon–Sat 10am–5pm (9am–7.30pm in Aug). Dominated by its towering black neo-Gothic spire, The Hub is the permanent headquarters of the Edinburgh International Festival (see p.176). The event itself takes place for three weeks each August and early September, but the Hub is open year-round, providing performance, rehearsal and exhibition spaces as well as a ticket centre, bookshop and café. The building was constructed in 1845 as an Assembly Hall for the Church of Scotland; its 1999 conversion introduced some radically colourful interiors and art installations. On the ground floor is the vivid yellow and electric blue interior of *Café Hub* (see p.78); also worth checking out is the main hall

upstairs, where the original woodwork and high-vaulted ceiling have been enlivened with a fabulous fabric design in Rastafarian colours, while on the main stairwell, 200 delightful foot-high sculptures depict Festival performers and audiences.

Gladstone's Land

477b Lawnmarket ☎0131/226 5856. Daily: April–Oct Mon–Sat 10am–5pm, Sun 2–5pm. £5. This tall, narrow building – not unlike a canalside house in Amsterdam – is the Royal Mile's best surviving example of a typical seventeenth century tenement. While it's not the Old Town's raciest attraction, the half-dozen rooms on show do offer a palpable sense of home life in medieval Edinburgh. The building is owned by the National Trust for Scotland, who have carefully restored the rooms, filling them with period furnishings and fittings; in each a prim guide is on hand to answer questions and pass out a sheet detailing what's on show. The six stories of the "land" would have been home to various families living one on top of each other – the well-to-do Gledstanes, who

PLACES The Royal Mile

▼INTERIOR ARTWORK, THE HUB

built it in 1620, are thought to have occupied the third floor. The arcaded and wooden-fronted ground floor is home to a reconstructed cloth shop; pass through this and you encounter a warren of tight little staircases, tiny rooms, creaking floorboards and peek-hole windows. The finest room, on the first floor immediately above the arcade, has a marvellous painted ceiling, some fine old dark furniture and an array of attractive rugs and Dutch paintings. The upper floors contain apartments which are rented to visitors (see p.159).

Writers' Museum

Lady Stair's Close ☎0131/529 4901, ⊛www.cac.org.uk. Mon–Sat 10am–5pm, plus Sun noon–5pm in Aug. Free. Tucked away in the charming Lady Stair's House – a Victorian embellishment of a seventeenth-century residence set to one side of an open courtyard – the Writers' Museum is dedicated to Scotland's three greatest literary lions, Sir Walter Scott, Robert Louis Stevenson and Robert Burns. Its slightly lacklustre collection includes portraits, manuscripts and showcases filled with odd knick-knacks and relics associated with the writers – Scott's walking stick and a plastercast of Burns' skull among them. Storyboards fill in the key details of the writers' lives and relationships with Edinburgh (Burns only ever made extended

visits to the city), and there are also brief displays on Scotland's other notable authors. The house itself holds as much interest as the exhibits, its tight, winding stairs and poky, wood-panelled rooms offering a flavour of the medieval Old Town. Known as the Makars' Court after the Scots word for the "maker" of poetry or prose, the courtyard outside continues the literary theme with a series of paving stones inscribed with quotations from Scotland's most famous writers and poets.

Parliament Square

The central section of the Royal Mile is dominated by the High Kirk of St Giles, the centrepiece of the cobbled Parliament Square. Three sides of this area (it's no longer strictly a square) are taken up with the Neoclassical facades of the Law Courts, originally designed by Robert Adam but completed by Robert Reid; his elevated Ionic columns and Classical statuary are typical of Edinburgh's grand Georgian style, but in fact the location is really too cramped for such flourishes to work effectively. Hidden behind the facade is the much older Parliament House, built in the 1630s for the then separate Scottish Parliament. After the move to Westminster in 1707, Parliament House was incorporated into the law courts, and its main feature, the impressive 122-foot long main hall, today acts as a grandiose lobby for the courtrooms beyond. As the courts are open to the public, it's possible to get inside to look at the hall (Mon–Fri 9am–5pm; free), with its extravagant hammerbeam roof and delicately carved stone corbels. In the far corner a small exhibition details the history of the building and courts, but it's more fun simply to watch everyday business going on in the hall, with solicitors and bewigged advocates in hushed conferrals, often following the time-honoured tradition of pacing up and down to prevent their conversation being overheard.

Elsewhere in Parliament Square, not far from the entrance to St Giles, is the Heart of Midlothian, a pattern set in the cobblestones which marks the site of the demolished tollbooth and prison; locals used to spit on the door of the prison to ward off the evil contained therein, and some still carry on the tradition today.

High Kirk of St Giles

Parliament Square ☏0131/225 9442, ⊛www.stgilescathedral.org.uk. Daily: May–Sept Mon–Fri 9am–7pm, Sat 9am–5pm, Sun 1–5pm; Oct–April Mon–Sat 9am–5pm, Sun 1–5pm.

Free. The original parish church of medieval Edinburgh, from where John Knox launched and directed the Scottish Reformation, St Giles is often referred to as a cathedral, although it has only been the seat of a bishop on two brief and unhappy occasions in the seventeenth century. Its location and historical significance mean that is often used for high-profile religious services, such as when the Queen is in town or at the opening of Parliament, though in fact it is strictly still an ordinary parish church with a regular congregation. The resplendent crown spire of the kirk is formed from eight flying buttresses and dates back to 1485, while inside, the four massive piers supporting the tower were part of a Norman church built here around 1120. In the nineteenth century, St Giles was adorned with a whole series of funerary monuments on the model of London's Westminster Abbey; around the same time it acquired several attractive Pre-Raphaelite stained-glass windows designed by Edward Burne-Jones and William Morris. At the southeastern corner of the interior, the Thistle Chapel was built by Sir Robert Lorimer in 1911 as the private chapel of the sixteen Knights of the Thistle, the highest chivalric order in Scotland. The compact structure is an exquisite piece of craftsmanship, with huge drooping bosses and extravagantly

▼HIGH KIRK OF ST GILES' EXTERIOR

ornate stalls showing off Lorimer's bold Arts and Crafts styling.

Mary King's Close

Warriston's Close ☏ 0870/243 0160, ⊛ www.realmarykingsclose.com. Daily: April–Oct 10am–9pm; Nov–March 10am–4pm; hour-long tours depart every 20min. £7. Running underneath the City Chambers (the home of Edinburgh's local government), Mary King's Close is one of the capital's most unusual attractions. When work on the chambers (initially designed to be a mercantile exchange) began in 1753, the existing tenements on the site were simply sliced through at the level of the High Street and the new building constructed on top of them. Because the tenements had been built on a steep hillside, this process left parts of the houses together with the old streets (or closes) which ran alongside them intact but entirely enclosed among the basement and cellars of the City Chambers. You can visit this rather spooky subterranean

▼ROYAL MILE SHOPPING

"lost city" on tours led by costumed actors, who take you round the old, cold stone shells of the houses where various scenes from the Close's history have been recreated. As you'd expect blood, plague, pestilence and ghostly apparitions are to the fore, though there is an acknowledgement of the more prosaic side of medieval life in the archeological evidence of an urban cow byre. The tour ends with a stroll up the remarkably well-preserved Mary King's Close itself.

Brass Rubbing Centre

Trinity Apse Church, Chalmers Close, High St ☏ 0131/556 4364, ⊛ www.cac .org.uk. April–Sept Mon–Sat 10am–5pm, plus Sun noon–5pm in Aug. Free. Tucked down a close off the Royal Mile, Trinity Apse is part of the fifteenth-century Trinity Collegiate Church which was reassembled on this spot after the original was demolished in 1845 to make way for Waverley railway station. Inside, a large variety of replica monumental brasses are available for making a rubbing, with the subject matter ranging from six-foot-tall medieval knights to swirling Pictish designs – all great fun for kids and adults alike.

Museum of Childhood

42 High St ☏ 0131/529 4142, ⊛ www .cac.org.uk. Mon–Sat 10am–5pm, plus Sun noon–5pm in July & Aug. Free. The Museum of Childhood has an odd history, having been founded in 1955 by a local councillor who heartily disliked children. In today's digital age the collection of dolls' houses, teddy bears, train sets and marionettes may be regarded as a little dull for some children, although their nostalgic charm often touches a chord with parents.

run-ins with Mary, Queen of Scots, a Catholic.

John Knox's House is linked to the Scottish Storytelling Centre, which is due to reopen in the summer of 2005 after a major redevelopment. The complex will include a theatre, café, story-telling garden and indoor story-telling court, with regular performances and events.

The People's Story

Canongate Tolbooth, 163 Canongate ☎0131/529 4057, ⊛www.cac.org .uk. Mon–Sat 10am–5pm, plus Sun noon–5pm in Aug only. Free. With its turreted steeple and box clock overhanging the street, the late sixteenth-century Canongate Tolbooth is a distinctive landmark halfway along the Canongate. It's occupied by a local history museum, the People's Story, which contains a series of display cases, dense information boards and rather old fashioned tableaux dedicated to the everyday life and work of Edinburgh's population down the centuries. This isn't one of Edinburgh's essential museums, but it does have a down-to-earth reality often missing from places dedicated to high culture or famous historical characters.

Museum of Edinburgh

Huntly House, 142 Canongate ☎0131/529 4143, ⊛www.cac.org .uk. Mon–Sat 10am–5pm, Sun noon–5pm (Aug only). Free. The city's principal collection devoted to local history, the Museum of Edinburgh is as interesting for the labyrinthine network of wood-panelled rooms within as for its rather quirky array of artefacts. These do, however, include a number of items of real historical significance, in particular the National Covenant, the petition for

▲JOHN KNOX'S HOUSE

John Knox's House

43–45 High St ⊛www .scottishstorytellingcentre.co.uk. Mon–Sat 10am–6pm, Sun noon–6pm. Closed for refurbishment until summer 2005; call ☎0131/556 9579 to confirm hours and entry fee. With its distinctive external staircase, clustered high chimneys and timber projections, this fifteenth-century building, popularly known as John Knox's House, is a classic representation of the Royal Mile in its medieval heyday. Inside the house is a museum about the building and in particular John Knox, the minister who led the Reformation in Scotland and established Calvinist Presbyterianism as the dominant religious force in the country. Popularly known as a tall, lean man with a long beard dressed in a flowing gown, preaching a stern, hard-line Protestant creed, Knox was the author of a religious tract titled *The First Blast of the Trumpet Against the Monstrous Regiment of Women*, and during his time in Edinburgh he famously had

▲CANONGATE KIRK

religious freedom drawn up on a deerskin parchment in 1638, and the original plans for the layout of the New Town drawn by James Craig (see p.110), chosen by the city council after a competition in 1767.

Canongate Kirk

Canongate. Mon–Sat 10.30am–4.30pm, depending on volunteer staff and services. Free. Constructed in the 1680s to house the congregation expelled from Holyrood Abbey when the latter was commandeered by James VII, Canongate Kirk has a modesty rarely seen in churches built in later centuries, with a graceful curved facade, arched and round windows and a bow-shaped gable to the rear. The airy interior has an odd light blue colour scheme, as well as various crests and flags that highlight the kirk's continuing royal and military connections. An attractive and tranquil stretch of green in the heart of the Old Town, the surrounding churchyard affords fine views up to Calton Hill; it also

happens to be one of the city's most exclusive cemeteries – well-known internees include the political economist Adam Smith, Mrs Agnes McLehose (better known as Robert Burns' "Clarinda") and Robert Fergusson, regarded by some as Edinburgh's greatest poet, despite his death at the age of 24 – his headstone was donated by Burns, a fervent admirer, who also wrote the inscription.

Dunbar's Close Garden

Dunbar's Close, Canongate. Unrestricted access. Free. A delightful discovery tucked in behind the high tenements of the Canongate, Dunbar's Close Garden is a lovely little green oasis formally laid out with gravel paths, yew hedges, beds of lavender and grassy squares in the style of a seventeenth-century Old Town garden. It's not hard to imagine how peaceful a space like this would have been, a world away from the hubbub of the cramped, dirty, bustling medieval city – these days it's a perfect haven if you're foot-weary from the tourist trail or simply looking for a tranquil spot to read a book or nibble a sandwich. A board mounted on one of the old ivy-covered walls states the garden was donated to the city (somewhat bizarrely) by the Mushroom Trust of Edinburgh in 1978.

Scottish Poetry Library

5 Crichton's Close, Canongate ☎0131/557 2876, ⊛www.spl.org .uk. Mon–Fri 11am–6pm, Sat 1–5pm. Free. Built in 1999, the Scottish Poetry Library is a small island of modern architectural and cultural eloquence amid a cacophony of recent

developments, most prominently the new Scottish Parliament. The building incorporates a section of an old city wall, and the attractive, thoroughly contemporary design harmoniously incorporates brick, oak, glass, Caithness stone and blue ceramic tiles. The library contains Scotland's most comprehensive collection of native poetry, and visitors are free to read the books, periodicals and leaflets found on the shelves, or listen to recordings of poetry in English, Scots and Gaelic. Readings and events are organized throughout the year.

Shops

Cadenhead's Whisky Shop
172 Canongate ☎0131/556 5864, ⊛www.wmcadenhead.com. Closed Sun. Founded in 1834, Cadenhead's looks fairly unassuming from the outside but stocks a vast range of spirits, with unique labels of gin and rum alongside a mind-boggling selection of independently bottled malt and blended whiskies.

Carson Clark Map Gallery
181–183 Canongate ☎0131/556 4710, ⊛www.carson-clark-gallery .co.uk. Closed Sun. A wonderful emporium of antique maps, charts and globes which relate mainly, but not exclusively, to Scotland.

Coda
12 Bank St ☎0131/622 7246. Just off the Royal Mile on the way down the Mound, Coda specializes in CDs of contemporary Scottish folk and roots music.

Corniche
2–4 Jeffrey St ☎0131/556 3707. Closed Sun. Long before designer labels became currency of the high street, this tiny place was a treasure-trove of ladies' designer labels from Katherine Hamnett to Jean Paul Gaultier. There's also a menswear section next door.

Geoffrey (Tailor) Kiltmakers
57–59 High St ☎0131/557 0256, ⊛www.geoffreykilts.co.uk. Probably the best of the Royal Mile's purveyors of kilts and associated paraphernalia, offering advice on getting kitted out in tartan and an outfit rental service. The shop is also famous for its "21st Century Kilts": designed as a fashion statement (with pockets for mobile phones) and made in materials such as leather, plain tweed and even camouflage.

Ness
367 High St ☎0131/226 5227, ⊛www .nessclothing.com. In the midst of dull woollen mill outlets, Ness

▼CARSON CLARK MAP GALLERY

▲COVERED CLOSE OFF THE ROYAL MILE

sells a range of refreshingly upbeat, contemporary modern Scottish designer knitwear and accessories.

Just Scottish

6 North Bank St, The Mound ☎0131/226 4807. One of the better places hereabouts to hunt down decent quality mainstream Scottish crafts, with painting, sculpture, ceramics and jewellery from some up-and-coming local artists.

Ragamuffin

278 Canongate ☎0131/557 6007, ⊕www.ragamuffinonline.co.uk. Open late on Thurs till 7pm. This vibrant, hippyish place selling designer knitwear and accessories in a burst of bright colours and groovy styles is an antidote to the beige V-neck sweaters piled high elsewhere on the Royal Mile.

Cafés

Always Sunday

170 High St ☎0131/622 0667. Proof that there's room for a bit of real food even on the tourist-thronged Royal Mile, this pleasantly positive independent café serves healthy lunches, homemade cakes, fresh smoothies and FairTrade coffee.

Café Hub

Lawnmarket ☎0131/473 2067. Radically coloured, well-run café in the Edinburgh Festival centre, with light modern meals served right through the day and most evenings, alongside teas, coffees, snacks and drinks. The large terrace is the best alfresco location on the Royal Mile.

Plaisir du Chocolat

251–253 Canongate ☎0131/556 9524. Unexpectedly classy Parisian-style tearoom serving delicious (if pricey) lunches, luxurious patisserie treats, and an array of gourmet teas and real hot chocolates.

Spoon

15 Blackfriars St ☎0131 556 6922. Down a side road off the High Street, and a world away from modern café blandness. The approach is simple, with short menus of imaginative soups, expertly crafted sandwiches and

a daily special such as farmhouse cheddar tart or boudin noir salad. Good coffee and cakes, too.

Restaurants

Amber

Scotch Whisky Heritage Centre, 354 Castlehill ☎0131/477 8477, ⊛www.amber-restaurant.co.uk. Neat, contemporary-styled place serving a good choice of light food such as potted shrimp at lunchtime, and more substantial and expensive dishes in the evenings (Thurs–Sat only), when there's a "whisky sommelier" on hand to suggest the best drams to accompany your honey-roast rack of Highland lamb or saddle of Balmoral venison.

Barioja

19 Jeffrey St ☎0131/557 3622. Closed Sun except in Aug. Open right

through the day and good for a lunchtime bocadillos sandwich or late-afternoon drink and snack, this Spanish-owned bar makes a decent stab at tapas in a metropolitan setting. Secure one of the few tables on the ground floor to get open views out to Calton Hill.

The Clamshell

148 High St ☎0131/225 4338. Fish and chips, albeit with few frills, on the busiest stretch of the Royal Mile – haggis, black pudding or steak pie suppers are also on offer.

David Bann's

56–58 St Mary's St ☎0131/556 5888, ⊛www.davidbann.com. Thoroughly modern vegetarian restaurant, open long hours and offering a wide choice of interesting, unconventional dishes such as courgette and sweetcorn fritters or celeriac and sweet potato roulade. The prices are very reasonable and the overall design is stylish and classy – not an open-toed sandal in sight.

La Garrigue

31 Jeffrey St ☎0131/557 3032, ⊛www.lagarrigue .co.uk. A place of genuine charm and quality, with a menu and wine list dedicated to the produce and traditions of the Languedoc region of France – the care and honesty of the cooking shines through in dishes such as cassoulet or bream with chard. Two courses at lunch are £10, rising to the £15-plus mark in the evening.

▼DAVID HUME STATUE, ROYAL MILE

Le Sept

5 Hunter Square ☎0131/225 5428,
ⓦwww.lesept.co.uk. Closed Sun
evening. Recently relocated but
long a reliable central option for
tasty, mid-priced French bistro
food, including savoury crepes
and daily-changing seafood
dishes.

Off the Wall

105 High St ☎0131/558 1497, ⓦwww
.off-the-wall.co.uk. Closed Sun except
during Aug. One of the best of
the upmarket restaurants on
the Royal Mile itself, with
a relatively unchallenging
atmosphere that belies some
seriously good modern Scottish
cooking. Expect to pay £15
for two courses at lunch, and
double that in the evening for
the likes of slow-roasted belly of
pork or hand-dived scallops.

Prego

38 St Mary's St ☎0131/557 5754,
ⓦwww.prego-restaurant.com. Closed
Sun. Classy but not overpriced
Italian place with a short,
confident seasonal menu (no
pizza) and knowledgeable
service. It's a bit like eating in
Italy, which is a rare find in
Britain.

Reform

267 Canongate ☎0131/558 9992,
ⓦwww.reformrestaurant.com.
Closed Sun. One of the first
places in Edinburgh to draw
strongly on the ideas of Pacific
Rim fusion food, this is a
fresh, imaginatively run place
which mixes the dignity of
the Old Town with a sense of
gastronomic adventure. Expect
to pay £14–19 for such dishes
as steamed snapper fillet or
barbecued ostrich steak with
pear chutney.

Viva Mexico

41 Cockburn St ☎0131/226 5145,
ⓦwww.viva-mexico.co.uk. Long one
of Edinburgh's best Mexican
restaurants, offering well-
executed staples in a friendly,
easy-going atmosphere.

The Witchery by the Castle

352 Castlehill ☎0131/225 5613,
ⓦwww.thewitchery.com. The
restaurant that only Edinburgh
could create, with Gothic
panelling, tapestries and heavy
stonework all a broomstick-hop
from the Castle. The grand fish
and game dishes are pricey, as
is the wine, but you can steal
a sense of it all with a pre- or
post-theatre set menu (£10).

Pubs and bars

Black Bo's

57–61 Blackfriars St. Daily 4pm–1am.
No music and no decent ales,
but a good example of how
to stay hip without going
minimalist, with church pews
and candles alongside original
art and DJ decks. Just fifty yards
from the Royal Mile, but well
off the tourist trail.

Deacon Brodie's Tavern

435 Lawnmarket. Daily 10am–1am. An
obvious historic pub, named after
the respectable late eighteenth-
century town councillor who
moonlighted as a burglar. He's
said to epitomize the duality of
Edinburgh's image as a dignified
professional city with a shadowy
underworld, and to have been
the inspiration for Stevenson's *Dr
Jekyll and Mr Hyde*.

EH1

197 High St. Daily 9am–1am. A
minimalist style-bar which
appears just at the point when
you're despairing of finding

cool aqua colours dominate, along with vividly coloured cocktails and some decent tunes.

Jolly Judge

7 James Court, Lawnmarket. Mon–Thurs 11am–11pm, Fri & Sat 11am–midnight. Atmospheric, low-ceilinged pub in an attractive courtyard off the Royal Mile. Cosy in winter, and pleasant outside in summer.

North Bridge

20 North Bridge. Sun–Thurs 11am–midnight, Fri & Sat 11am–1am. Plush in-hotel cocktail bar, with its slick glass island bar contrasting with ornate pillars and original panelling. Good-quality food is served at intimate tables for two on the encircling balcony.

▲DEACON BRODIE FIGURE, ROYAL MILE

a pub that Rabbie Burns or Bonnie Prince Charlie didn't drink in. Wrought iron and

Holyrood and Arthur's Seat

Holyrood is home to three dramatically contrasting elements of Edinburgh: medieval history, in the royal palace of Holyroodhouse and its ruined thirteenth-century abbey; sensational modern architecture, in the form of Enric Miralles' dazzling but highly controversial new Scottish Parliament; and an invigorating blast of the great outdoors, in the cliffs and ridges of Edinburgh's most dramatic natural feature, the old royal hunting ground of Holyrood Park and its slumbering peak, Arthur's Seat. As a result, the area has an intensity and a sense of escapism which, when wrapped up together, can provide some slightly surreal moments, with groups of royalist tourists shuffling past a huddle of republican-minded politicians, or sharp-suited civil servants hurrying by cagoul-clad outdoor types setting out for Salisbury Crags.

Palace of Holyroodhouse

Main entrance from Horse Wynd ☎0131/556 5100, ⊛www.royal.gov .uk. Daily: Nov–March 9.30am–4.30pm; April–Oct 9.30am–6pm. £8 or £11 joint ticket with the Queen's Gallery. Holyrood became established as Edinburgh's main royal quarters during the reigns of James V and of his daughter Mary, Queen of Scots, who favoured it over the draughty castle. A century later Charles II's architects transformed it into one of the finest Scottish buildings of the age, but it wasn't until Queen Victoria's reign that a monarch travelled to Scotland frequently enough to establish an official residence. Visits by the Queen are common today (the palace is therefore closed in mid May, late June and mid November), and

▼PALACE OF HOLYROODHOUSE

▲ PALACE GATES, HOLYROOD

secretary, David Rizzio, was dragged in 1566 by conspirators who included her jealous husband, Lord Darnley; a brass plaque in the outer chamber is said to mark bloodstains on the wooden floor where Rizzio was stabbed 56 times.

Holyrood Abbey

Access as part of Holyroodhouse tour (see above). Immediately adjacent to the palace are the poignant ruins of Holyrood Abbey, some of which date to the thirteenth century. Various invading armies paid little respect to the building over the years, and although it was patched up for Charles I's coronation in 1633 it was gutted in 1688 by an anti-Catholic mob. The roof finally tumbled down in 1768, but the melancholy scene has inspired artists down the years, among them Felix Mendelssohn, who in 1829 wrote "Everything is in ruins and mouldering . . . I believe I have found the beginning of my Scottish Symphony there today". Adjacent to the abbey are the formal palace gardens, open to visitors during the summer months and offering some pleasant short strolls.

Queen's Gallery

Horse Wynd ☎0131/556 5100, ✆www .royal.gov.uk. April–Oct 9.30am–6pm; Nov–March 9.30am–4.30pm. £5 or £11 joint ticket with Holyroodhouse. Essentially an adjunct to Holyrood palace, the Queen's Gallery is located in the shell of a former church directly between the palace and the parliament. With just two principal viewing rooms, it's a compact space, but has an appealing contemporary style which manages to remain sympathetic to the older

are invariably surrounded by a great rousing of the nobility in Scotland as well as plenty of pomp and ceremony.

Compared to most royal palaces, visitor access to Holyroodhouse is extensive. A series of royal reception rooms feature some outstanding encrusted plasterwork, each more impressive than the last – an idea Charles II had picked up from his cousin Louis XIV's Versailles – while on the opposite side of the internal quadrangle, the Great Gallery extends almost the full length of the palace and is dominated by portraits of 96 Scottish kings, painted by Jacob de Wet in 1684. It was a ridiculous commission by Charles II with laughable results: the compliant De Wet ensured that the Stewart family's facial characteristics prevailed all the way back to Fergus I. Just beyond this, in the oldest part of the palace, the formal, ceremonial tone gives way to dark medieval history, with a tight spiral staircase leading to the chambers used by Mary, Queen of Scots. These contain various relics associated with the queen, though the most compelling viewing is a tiny supper room, from where Mary's Italian

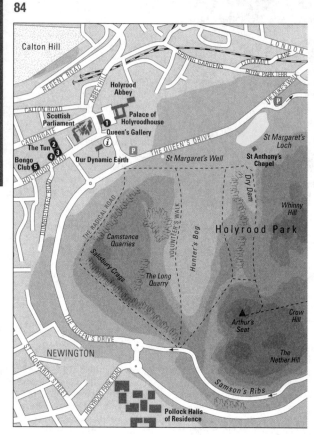

elements of the building. It's used to display changing exhibitions from the Royal Collection, a vast array of art treasures held by the Queen on behalf of the British nation. Because the pieces are otherwise exhibited only during the limited openings of Buckingham and Windsor palaces, the exhibitions here tend to draw quite a lot of interest. Recent displays have included a priceless collection of drawings by Leonardo da Vinci and a glittering array of jewellery by Russian goldsmith Carl Fabergé.

The Scottish Parliament

Horse Wynd ☎0131/348 5000, ⊛www .scottish.parliament.uk. Business days (normally Tues–Thurs) 9am–7pm; non-business days (normally Mon & Fri–Sun, or Mon–Sun if Parliament is in recess) 10am–4pm. Free entrance to debating chamber and lobby; full guided tours £3.50. By far the most controversial public building to be erected in Scotland since the Second World War, Scotland's unusual new parliament building is the home of the country's directly elected assembly, which was re-established in 1999. Initial estimates for the building, constructed on the site of a

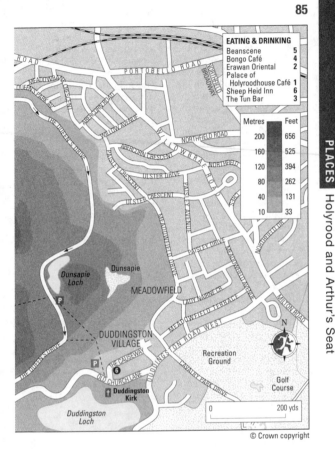

EATING & DRINKING

Beanscene	5
Bongo Café	4
Erawan Oriental	2
Palace of Holyroodhouse Café	1
Sheep Heid Inn	6
The Tun Bar	3

disused brewery at the foot of the Royal Mile, were tentatively (and rashly) put at £40 million; by the time the Queen cut the ribbon to open the doors, the final bill was in the region of £450 million. The unique design is the vision of Catalan architect Enric Miralles, whose death in 2000 caused more than a few ripples of uncertainty as to whether the famously whimsical designer had in fact set down his final vision. There are six interlinked structures within the complex, among them Queensberry House, which

▼SCOTTISH PARLIAMENT EXTERIOR

dates back to 1681, and the rather more modernistic towers housing offices and committee rooms. Miralles had a conviction that "the Parliament sits in the land", which helps explain the leaf or petal-shaped design of the central buildings. This is just one of a number of motifs and odd shapes which run through the design, including the anvil-like shape which clads the exterior of the building, and the extraordinary windows of the MSPs' offices, shaped like the profile of a mountain or a section of the Forth Rail Bridge and said to have been inspired by a monk's contemplative cell. The main debating chamber is grand yet intimate and undoubtedly contemporary, with light flooding in through high windows and a complex network of thick oak beams. The other part of the building generally open to the public is the entrance lobby; a small exhibition here provides some historical, political and architectural background to the parliament. However, for a better appreciation of the quality and detail of design, which seems to have been brought to every nook and cranny of the complex, it's well worth joining one of the guided tours which allow visitors a peek at the dramatic committee rooms with their views of Salisbury Crags, the glass-roofed garden lobby and the MSPs' wood-lined offices.

Our Dynamic Earth

Holyrood Rd ☎0131/550 7800, ⊛www.dynamicearth.co.uk. April–June, Sept–Oct daily 10am–5pm; July–Aug daily 10am–6pm; Nov–March Wed–Sun 10am–5pm. £8.95. Laid out beneath a pincushion of white metal struts, this modern, hi-tech attraction based on the wonders of the natural world is principally aimed at families with kids between five and fifteen. Inside, a "time machine" elevator whisks you off to the creation of the universe, fifteen billion years ago, which is described using impressive wide-screen video graphics, eerie music and a deep-throated commentary. Subsequent galleries cover the formation of the earth and continents with crashing sound effects and a shaking floor, while the calmer grandeur of glaciers and oceans is explored through magnificent large-screen landscape footage. The "Casualties and Survivors" gallery illustrates the history of life on earth, from primordial swamps to life-size models of some of the odd creatures who once inhabited the earth; further on, the polar regions – complete with a real iceberg – and tropical jungles are imaginatively re-created, with interactive computer screens and special effects at every turn. Outside,

▼OUR DYNAMIC EARTH

▲SWANS ON DUDDINGSTON LOCH

the dramatic amphitheatre which incorporates the steps leading up to the main entrance serves as a great venue for outdoor theatre and music performances, most notably during the Festival.

Holyrood Park

Unrestricted access. A large area of parkland and rough hillside immediately to the south of the palace and new parliament, the former royal hunting ground of Holyrood Park is one of Edinburgh's greatest assets, a 650-acre swathe of rock, hill and moor which brings a taste of Highland wildness into the centre of the city. While old photographs of the park show crops growing and sheep grazing, it's now most heavily used by walkers, joggers, cyclists and other outdoor enthusiasts. A single tarred road, the Queen's Drive, loops through the park, enabling many of its features to be seen by car – however, you need to get out and stroll around to appreciate it fully. Following Queen's Drive in a clockwise direction from the palace gates, you'll arrive at St Margaret's Loch, a nineteenth-century man-made pond, above which stand the simple ruins of St Anthony's Chapel. From here, the road around the back of Arthur's Seat is one-

way only for vehicular traffic, and ascends to Dunsapie Loch, tucked in below the summit. If you're on foot and feeling reasonably intrepid, you can tackle the various paths that criss-cross the park, though decent walking shoes, a waterproof and drinking water are recommended. You can pick up a map of suggested walks, as well as weekly ranger-led walks, from the Royal Parks Constabulary Portakabin in the car park situated between the palace and Salisbury Crags.

Salisbury Crags

Holyrood Park. Unrestricted access. A curve of red cliffs stretching from above Holyrood Palace to the steep north side of Arthur's Seat, Salisbury Crags are the face of an angled dolerite sill of hard teschenite rock which once lay under the volcanic deposits that form most of the rest of the park. From his observations here in the late seventeenth century, James Hutton, widely regarded as the father of geology, was able to establish his (then) radical theories about the age of the earth and its features. A path, known as the Radical Road after the unemployed "radicals" given the task of building it in the 1820s, follows the base of the crags and is arguably a finer walk than the sharper climb to the top of Arthur's Seat. As the path rises the city gradually reveals itself, the lower perspective of the crags clearly showing the dominance of Castle Rock and the ridge

▲ RADICAL ROAD, SALISBURY CRAGS

in Holyrood Park is to walk around the Queen's Drive to Dunsapie Loch, from where it's a twenty-minute climb up grassy slopes to the rocky summit. On a clear day, the views might just stretch to the English border and the Atlantic Ocean; more realistically, the landmarks which dominate are Fife, a few Highland peaks and, of course, Edinburgh laid out on all sides.

down which the Royal Mile runs. Note that climbing is not allowed on the crags, and that there's no continuous path along the top of the crags; an exploration here is dangerous, particularly in wet, windy or misty conditions. A better looped walk of about an hour's duration from Holyrood is to follow the "Volunteer's Walk" up the glen behind the Crags, then return along the Radical Road.

Arthur's Seat

Holyrood Park. Unrestricted access. At 823 feet above sea level, the summit of Arthur's Seat easily overreaches all of Edinburgh's numerous high points. Part of a volcano which last saw action 350 million years ago, its connections to the legendary Celtic king are fairly sketchy: the name is likely to be a corruption of the Gaelic *Ard-na-said*, or "height of arrows". The simplest and safest approach to the top from most points

Duddingston Loch and Village

Holyrood Park's only natural stretch of water, Duddingston Loch often freezes over in winter and is perhaps best known as the location for the famous portrait of "the skating minister", one of the best-loved paintings displayed at the National Gallery (see p.107). Today it operates as a bird sanctuary (free access) with swans, herons and grebes often seen around its reedy fringes. Perched above the loch, just outside the park boundary, Duddingston Kirk dates back in part to the twelfth century and lies at the heart of Duddingston Village, an unspoilt corner of the city with cobbled lanes, cute cottages and, inevitably, high price tags. The *Sheep Heid Inn* here (see p.89) is one of Edinburgh's oldest pubs and a great waypoint if you're exploring the park; out at the back of the pub there's a traditional skittle alley, still very much in working order.

Cafés

Beanscene

67 Holyrood Rd. ⊛www.beanscene
.com. Part of a Scottish mini-
chain where the emphasis is on
coffee in a relaxed, smoke-free,
child-friendly environment.
Tapas-like snacks are available,
the doors shut at 11pm nightly,
and there's often good music
either on the sound system or
live on certain nights.

Bongo Café

37 Holyrood Rd. Closed Sun. Grungy
but hip alternative café, linked
to the nightclub of the same
name (see p.173), with a simple
menu of wraps and toasted
panini with good coffee and
homemade cakes; there's art on
the walls, free internet access
and meaningful music.

Palace of Holyroodhouse Café

Holyrood Mews (enter via Queen's
Gallery entrance or Abbey Strand).
Given the dearth of decent
eating places in the Holyrood
quarter, this is a good option
for lunch or a coffee, with
sandwiches and hot daily
specials featuring produce from
the Windsor Farm Shop. Sit
inside in a pleasant glasshouse-
style area, or outside in a garden
space with views of the Crags.
You don't need a ticket for the
palace or gallery to get in.

Restaurants

Erawan Oriental

Unit 4, The Tun, Holyrood Rd
☏0131/556 242. One of a small
local chain of Thai restaurants,
this branch successfully mixes
its cool modern setting with
traditional elements of decor.
The moderately priced menu
manages a similar balance,
with most of the old favourites
alongside fried snapper with
mango, or Indonesian satays.

Pubs and bars

Sheep Heid Inn

43 The Causeway, Duddingston.
Mon–Wed & Sat–Sun 11am–11pm,
Thurs & Fri 11am–midnight. One of
Edinburgh's best-known historic
pubs, the building has barely
survived various predictable
makeovers, but despite this it
remains an attractive spot. The
food is decent without troubling
the gastropub inspectors.

The Tun Bar

Holyrood Rd. Mon–Sat 11am–11pm, Sun
noon–6pm. Located in the ground
floor of the angular, all-glass
Tun building, this is a popular
meeting point for journalists and
politicians who have been prised
out of the parliament's in-house
canteens. Standing room only
after work; at other times you
might find a chocolate-coloured
sofa to sink into.

▼SKITTLE ALLEY, SHEEP HEID INN

South of the Royal Mile

The section of the Old Town immediately south of the Royal Mile operates, quite literally, on two levels. On the upper tier, the elevated viaducts of George IV Bridge and South Bridge connect the Royal Mile with the city's university precinct, where a youthful, studenty atmosphere intertwines with the cultural tone provided by Edinburgh's two principal history museums. Below runs the Cowgate, overshadowed by the tall buildings on either side but busy with clubbers after dark; and the more open Grassmarket, a former execution site that's now home to closely packed pubs, restaurants and boutique shops.

National Library of Scotland

George IV Bridge ☎ 0131/2264531, ⓦ www.nls.uk. Mon, Tues, Thurs & Fri 9.30am–8.30pm, Wed 10am–8.30pm, Sat 9.30am–1pm. Free. A looming, windowless facade staring out blankly from the east side of George IV Bridge, the National Library's bare classicism is a little forbidding, though it's worth stepping back to admire the allegorical figures by Scottish sculptor Hew Lorimer which decorate the exterior. This is Scotland's largest library and one of the UK's copyright libraries (it holds a copy of every book published in the country), and you have to apply for a readers' ticket to gain access to the collection. However, the interesting, well-researched small exhibitions on the subject of books, printing and the written word (mounted in a side gallery on the ground floor) offer the chance of a peek inside the building.

▼STYLISED FIGURES, NATIONAL LIBRARY FACADE

Grassmarket

An open, partly cobbled area girdled by tall tenements, the Grassmarket was used as the city's cattle market from 1477 to 1911. Despite the height of many of the surrounding buildings, it offers an unexpected view up to the precipitous crags of the Castle and, come springtime, it's sunny enough for cafés to put tables and chairs along the pavement. Such continental aspirations are a bit misleading, however, as the Grassmarket is best remembered as the location of Edinburgh's public gallows – the spot is marked by a tiny garden. It was also the scene of the city's best-known civic uprising in

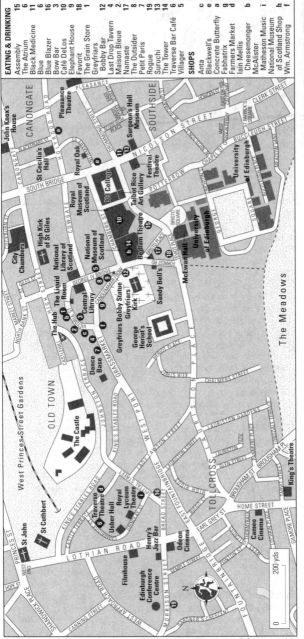

EATING & DRINKING

Assembly	15
The Atrium	6
Black Medicine	11
Blue	6
Blue Blazer	16
Bow Bar	3
Café DeLos	10
Elephant House	9
Favorit	18
The Grain Store	1
Greyfriars	
Bobby Bar	12
Last Drop Tavern	4
Maison Bleue	2
Namaste	17
The Outsider	8
Petit Paris	7
Rogue	19
Suruchi	13
The Tower	14
Traverse Bar Café	6
Villager	5

SHOPS

Anta	c
Blackwell's	e
Concrete Butterfly	a
Fabhatrix	g
Farmers Market	d
Iain Mellis	b
Cheesemonger	
McAlister	
Matheson Music	i
National Museum	h
of Scotland Shop	
Wm. Armstrong	f

© Crown copyright

▲MEMORIALS, GREYFRIARS KIRK

Bobby Bar (see p.101), Greyfriars Kirkyard has a fine collection of seventeenth-century gravestones and mausoleums, including one to the Adam family of architects. The kirkyard is visited regularly by ghost tours (see p.69) and was known for grave-robbing long before Burke and Hare became the city's most notorious exponents of the crime. Bizarrely, as recently as 2004 two youths were tried at the High Court under the ancient laws of "desecration of a sepulchre", after they broke into one of the mausoleums and were spotted playing with a skull. More significantly, the kirkyard was the setting, in 1638, for the signing of the National Covenant, a dramatic act of defiance by the Presbyterian Scots against the attempts of Charles I to impose an Episcopal form of worship on the country. In an undemocratic age, thousands of townsfolk as well as important nobles signed the original at Greyfriars; copies were then made and sent around the country with some 300,000 names being added.

1736, when the Captain of the Town Guard, John Porteous, was dragged from the Tolbooth and lynched by a mob upset that he had escaped punishment after ordering the Guard to shoot into a potentially restless execution crowd; nine citizens were killed. The notorious duo William Burke and William Hare had their lair in a now-vanished close just off the western end of the Grassmarket, and for a long time before its relatively recent gentrification there was a seamy edge to the place, with brothels, drinking dens and shelters for down-and-outs. Tucked away in the northwest corner is the award winning modern architecture of **Dance Base** ☎0131/225 5525, ⊛www.dancebase.co.uk), Scotland's National Centre for Dance, where classes, workshops and shows are held. Elsewhere, the Grassmarket's row of history-themed pubs have become a focus for many of the stag and hen parties which descend on Edinburgh, and there's also a series of interesting shops, in particular the string of offbeat, independent boutiques on Victoria Street.

Greyfriars Kirk and Kirkyard

Candlemaker Row. ⊛www .greyfriarskirk.com. Entered by a gateway beside *Greyfriars*

Greyfriars Kirk itself was built in 1620 on land which had belonged to a Franciscan convent, though little of the original late-Gothic style building remains. A fire in the mid-nineteenth century led to significant rebuilding and the installation of the first organ in a Presbyterian church in

Scotland; today's magnificent instrument, by Peter Collins, arrived in 1990.

Greyfriars Bobby Statue

George IV Bridge. For all Greyfriars' rich history, the kirkyard's international renown stems mostly from a scruffy wee Skye terrier, Bobby, who was owned by a police constable named John Gray. When Gray died in 1858, Bobby was found a few days later sitting on his grave, a vigil he maintained until his death fourteen years later. In the process, he became an Edinburgh celebrity, fed and cared for by locals who gave him a special collar to prevent him being impounded as a stray. A statue was modelled from life and erected soon after his death; it's located just outside the kirkyard opposite the pub bearing the dog's name. Bobby's legendary dedication easily lent itself to sentimental children's books and was eventually picked up by Disney, whose 1960 feature film hammed up the story and ensured that streams of tourists have paid their respects ever since.

George Heriot's School

Lauriston Place ⊛www.george-heriots.com. The impressive four-turreted George Heriot's Hospital, often mistaken for Holyrood palace, is now one of Edinburgh's most prestigious fee-paying schools. Founded as a home for poor boys by "Jinglin' Geordie" Heriot, James VI's goldsmith, its array of towers, turrets, chimneys, carved doorways and traceried windows are one of the finest achievements of the seventeenth-century Scottish Renaissance. While you can't go inside, it's possible to enter the grounds during school holidays (via the gates on Lauriston Place) and take a stroll around the outside of the building and the interior quadrangle to admire the architectural finery from up close.

National Museum of Scotland

Chambers St ☏0131/247 4422, ⊛www.nms.ac.uk. Mon & Wed–Sat 10am–5pm, Tues 10am–8pm, Sun noon–5pm. Free. Scotland's premier museum, the National displays many of the nation's most important historical artefacts as a means of telling the nation's history from earliest man to the present day. The striking honey-coloured sandstone structure was custom-built in the 1990s, its modern lines and imaginatively designed interior offering a fresh – but still respectful – perspective on the nation's story and its historic treasures. The cylindrical entrance tower, with its echoes of Edinburgh Castle, has a doorway at its base which leads to the soaring central lobby, Hawthornden Court; from here, you can join one of the

PLACES South of the Royal Mile

▼CRAMOND LIONESS, NATIONAL MUSEUM OF SCOTLAND

free guided tours on different themes that depart throughout the day, or pick up an audio headset (also free) which provides detailed information on the displays. The collection is generally, though not strictly, laid out in chronological order over seven different levels. The labyrinthine feel of the rooms and stairways is a little disorienting at first, though the unexpected views of different parts of the museum above and below are a deliberate effect by the architect to emphasize the interconnectedness of the layers of Scotland's history.

Some of the most precious artefacts are found in the galleries covering Scotland's earliest people on Level 0; these include the Trappain treasure hoard of silver plates, cutlery and goblets, and the Cramond Lioness, a sculpture from a Roman tombstone found recently in the Firth of Forth. Various contemporary artworks here, including pieces by Edinburgh-born sculptor Sir Eduardo Paolozzi and environmental artist Andy Goldsworthy, complement the historical items.

The scarcity of remains from the medieval period make levels 1 and 2 less cluttered than the upper floors, and both the Monymusk reliquary, an intricately decorated box said to have carried the remains of St Columba, and the delightful Lewis chessmen, exquisitely idiosyncratic twelfth-century pieces carved from walrus ivory, stand out in splendid isolation. The higher up you go, the more recent the history – the exhibits culminate in a twentieth-century gallery on Level 6. Above this is a small roof garden, accessed by a lift, which affords some great vistas of the city. Other fine views can be enjoyed from the museum's stylish *Tower* restaurant (see p.100).

Royal Museum of Scotland

Chambers St ☏0131/247 4422, ⊛www.nms.ac.uk. Mon & Wed–Sat 10am–5pm, Tues 10am–8pm, Sun noon–5pm. Free. Next door to and interlinked with the National Museum (though with a separate entrance), this dignified Venetian-style palace from the 1860s is a wonderful example of Victorian Britain's fascination with antiquities and natural history. Its exhibits are extraordinarily eclectic, from butterfly collections to colonial loot – ranging around the world and through many different aspects of science, history, design and nature. The wonderfully airy Great Hall, framed in cast-iron in the model of the Crystal Palace in London, holds sculpture from Classical

▼WHALE SKELETON, ROYAL MUSEUM OF SCOTLAND

▲OLD COLLEGE DOME

Greece and Rome alongside Buddhas from Japan, a totem pole from British Columbia and the bizarre Millennium Clock, a ten-metre tall, Heath-Robinson-style contraption which clicks and whirls into motion at 11am, noon, 2pm and 4pm. Rooms leading off from here hold collections of stuffed animals and birds, including the full skeleton of a blue whale. The more specialized collections on the upper floors include Egyptian mummies, ceramics from ancient Greece to the present day, and a splendid selection of European decorative art.

Old College

South Bridge ⊛www.ed.ac.uk. The oldest remaining part of the University of Edinburgh, the Old College was founded as the "Tounis College" in 1583 by James VI; it's now Scotland's largest university, with nearly 20,000 full-time students and an expansive campus which covers much of the area between here and the north edge of the Meadows

(see p.145). The original plan for the Old College came courtesy of Robert Adam, and work on his magnificent vaulted entrance of monolithic Roman Doric columns began in 1789. Adam's death in 1792 and the Napoleonic Wars halted progress, and the college was completed in 1816 in a considerably modified form by William Playfair, whose splendid 138 foot-long Upper Library, now known as the Playfair Library, is one of the city's finest Neoclassical rooms. Housing offices and the law faculty, The Old College is still a working part of the university, though as a spectacle it suffers from the fact that the traffic and houses of South Bridge close in too much to allow you a proper perspective of Adam's facade. For a fuller sense of the building, wander into the internal quadrangle; it's also sometimes possible for visitors to have a look around the interior of the Playfair Library – ask at the reception on the ground floor (or phone ☎0131/650 2093).

Talbot Rice Art Gallery

Old College, South Bridge ☎0131/650 2211, ⊛www.trg.ed.ac.uk. Tues–Sat 10am–5pm, plus Sun 10am–5pm in Aug only. Free. The small Talbot Rice Art Gallery displays, in rather lacklustre fashion, some of the University's large art and bronze collection, including a number of twentieth-century works by Scots Joan Eardley and William McTaggart. The main reason to head here, however, are the avant garde touring and temporary exhibitions which are mounted on a regular basis – the show held during the Festival is normally of a high standard.

Burke and Hare

The story of Burke and Hare ranks as the most notorious of the dark deeds associated with Edinburgh's Old Town. In the early 1800s the anatomy classes at Edinburgh's medical school were constantly seeking bodies for dissection, which meant good business for bodysnatchers who would illegally dig up freshly interred corpses from the city's graveyards. Two Irish immigrants to the city, William Burke and William Hare, took to simply murdering travellers, waifs and strays – people no-one would miss – and selling them to the school's anatomy professor. Their victims numbered into the teens before they were rumbled; Hare turned king's evidence and Burke was convicted of the murders. He was hanged in the High Street before a crowd of 25,000 and, inevitably, his body was given to the medical school for dissection.

Surgeons' Hall Museum

Surgeons' Hall, Nicolson St ☎0131/527 1649, ⊛www.rcsed .ac.uk. Mon–Fri noon–4pm; call or check website for details of extended opening hours from summer 2005 onward. Free. This handsome Ionic temple built in 1832 by William Playfair as the home of Edinburgh's Royal College of Surgeons houses one of the city's most unusual and morbidly compelling museums. In the eighteenth and nineteenth century Edinburgh developed as a leading centre for medical and anatomical research, nurturing world-famous pioneers such as James Young Simpson, founder of anaesthesia, and Joseph Lister, the father of modern surgery. The history of surgery takes up one part of the museum, with intriguing exhibits ranging from early surgical tools to a pocketbook covered with the leathered skin of bodysnatcher William Burke (see above). Another room has an array of gruesome instruments illustrating the history of dentistry; nearby is a small display dedicated to a past president of the college, Joseph Bell, whose diagnostic prowess was immortalized by one of his students, Arthur Conan Doyle, who based his famous detective Sherlock Holmes on Bell. The third and most remarkable part of the museum, the elegant Playfair Hall, is due to be opened fully to the public in July 2005, as part of the quincentenary of the college, and contains a remarkable array of specimens and jars from the college's

▼UNIVERSITY BUILDINGS, BRISTO SQUARE

anatomical and pathological collections dating back to the eighteenth century. A vital aid to teaching in those days, the rows of glass jars contain every conceivable body part in various states of repair, along with an equally stomach-churning but compelling array of bones, skeletons and graphic paintings illustrating war wounds from the Battle of Waterloo.

Shops

Anta

1–93 West Bow (Victoria St) ⓣ0131/226 4616, ⓦwww.anta.co.uk. Three floors of Anta's distinctive designs, which offer an original contemporary adaptation of the tartan and tweed image – rugs, throws, curtains, bags and ceramics in muted but stylish styles and tones.

Blackwell's

53–62 South Bridge ⓣ0131/622 8222, ⓦwww.blackwell.co.uk. One of the city's larger bookshops, with a good range of titles relating to Edinburgh and Scotland. It's open on weekdays until 8pm, there's a *Caffe Nero* tacked on the side, and the numerous nooks, crannies and floors give it a cosy, quasi-academic feel.

Concrete Butterfly

317–319 Cowgate ⓣ0131/558 7130. Closed Sun & Mon. Funky

modern accessories and designer household items by interesting European and Scottish designers. Next door, Concrete Wardrobe has some stylish women's clothing.

Fabhatrix

13 Cowgatehead ⓣ0131 225 9222, ⓦwww.fabhatrix.com. A modern hat shop, at once funky and fashionable, with some seriously cool designs in felt or silk from £25. Good if there's a chilly wind blowing or you're going to Ascot.

Farmers' Market

Castle Terrace, ⓣ0131/652 5940, ⓦwww.edinburghcc.com. First and third Sat of every month 9am–2pm. Meat, fish, vegetables, fruit, cheese and bread, much of it organic, sold direct by farmers from around the Lothians, Fife and the Borders.

Iain Mellis Cheesemonger

30a Victoria St ⓣ0131/226 6215, ⓦwww.ijmellischeesemonger.com. A cramped, pungent shop on colourful Victoria Street with rounds of British and Irish farmhouse cheeses piled alongside a perfectly matured selection from the Continent.

McAlister Matheson Music

1 Grindlay St ⓣ0131/2283827, ⓦwww.mmmusic.co.uk. Closed Sun. The most pleasant and informed place to buy classical CDs

---

Edinburgh's theatreland

The small area under the western lee of Castle Rock, between the Grassmarket and Lothian Road, acts as a focus of Edinburgh's cultural life in the eleven months outside August's Festival. Here you'll find the circular Usher Hall, venue for major orchestral performances as well as middle-of-the-road rock and pop concerts; the Royal Lyceum Theatre, for mainstream theatre; the Traverse, one of Britain's leading venues for avant-garde theatre and new writing; and the Filmhouse, the city's principal arthouse cinema. For more on all of these venues, see Essentials, p.172.

▲WM. ARMSTRONG

in Edinburgh, with a decent selection of jazz and Scottish folk as well.

National Museum of Scotland Shop

National Museum of Scotland, Chambers St ☎0131/247 4422. One of Edinburgh's better showcases for quality modern Scottish crafts and jewellery, as well as tasteful gifts inspired by the museum's collection, and instructive children's toys and games.

Wm. Armstrong

83 Grassmarket ☎0131/220 5557. A wonderful emporium of secondhand clothing, from sixties floral dresses to brass-buttoned military jackets with brass buttons.

Cafés

Black Medicine Coffee Company

2 Nicolson Street ☎0131/622 7209. Closed Sun. Just opposite the Old College, with chunky wooden furniture and the usual array of coffees, cakes and lunchtime platters.

Café DeLos

Royal Museum of Scotland, 2 Chambers St ☎0131/247 4111. The menu may not be startlingly imaginative, but the setting is a winner, right in the middle of the soaring, echoing atrium of the Royal Museum.

Elephant House

21 George IV Bridge ☎0131/220 5355. Slated as one of the places where J.K. Rowling, then a hard-up single mum, nursed her cups of coffee while penning the first Harry Potter novel, this is a decent daytime and evening café with a terrific room at the back full of philosophizing students and visitors peering dreamily at the views of the Castle.

Favorit

19–20 Teviot Place ☎0131/220 6880. Slick, modern café-diner in chrome and neon, dishing up coffees, fruit shakes and big sandwiches, as well as alcohol, right through to the wee small hours, making it a hit with the post-club crowd.

Restaurants

The Atrium
10 Cambridge St ℡ 0131/228 8882, ⌨ www.atriumrestaurant.co.uk. Closed Sat lunch and Sun. One of the most consistently impressive of Edinburgh's top-end restaurants. Quirky, arty design features include railway-sleeper tables, while the food focuses on high-quality Scottish produce such as carpaccio of Buccleuch beef, or warm berries served with mascarpone sorbet.

blue
10 Cambridge St ℡ 0131/221 1222, ⌨ www.bluebarcafe.com. Closed Sun. With minimalist modern decor, this impressive café/bistro hits the spot in terms of standards of food and service. It's handy for a quality pre- or post-theatre bite, with tasty modern dishes such as sea bass and tapenade or confit duck leg with champ for under £10, and is one of the city's more sophisticated child-friendly options.

The Grain Store
30 Victoria St ℡ 0131/225 7635, ⌨ www.grainstore-restaurant.co.uk. This unpretentious restaurant is a relaxing haven above the bustle of the Old Town, serving fairly uncomplicated but top-quality modern Scottish food

such as saddle of venison with beetroot fondant or toasted goat's cheese with caramelized walnuts. Reasonable lunchtime and set-price options.

Maison Bleue
36–38 Victoria St ℡ 0131/226 1900, ⌨ www.maison-bleue.co.uk. A contemporary bistro with an eclectic menu of tapas-style food such as calamari, Merguez sausages or haggis balls in beer batter. The lunch and early evening menus are good value.

Namaste
15 Bristo Place ℡ 0131/225 2000. Closed Sat & Sun lunch. A simple Indian diner in student-land with attractive Indian furniture and artefacts. The menu is (unusually) limited to two sides of paper, and dishes such as minty pudini chicken are light, tasty and beautifully cooked in a traditional brass pot.

The Outsider
15–16 George IV Bridge ℡ 0131/226 3131. Style conscious, arty modern restaurant open right through from lunch to late evening and permanently filled with beautiful young things. The food, which leans towards fish, salads and healthier options, is fresh, modern, informal and, surprisingly, not overpriced.

▼ THE OUTSIDER

▲PETIT PARIS DELIVERY VAN

Petit Paris

38–40 Grassmarket ☎0131/226 2442,
🌐www.petitparis-restaurant.co.uk. Daily
noon–11pm. Pleasingly realistic
French bistro, coupling a sincere
attitude with tasty Gallic nosh,
including good plat du jour
deals. The best dishes – slow-
baked rabbit saddle, perhaps, or
coq au vin à l'ancienne – are
scribbled in indecipherable text
on the blackboard, and there's
outside seating.

Suruchi

14a Nicolson St ☎0131/556 6583,
🌐www
.suruchirestaurant
.co.uk. Closed Sun lunch. Popular
establishment serving genuine
South Indian dishes, though the
menu is written in bizarre but
entertaining broad Scots. Look
out for cross-cultural specials
such as tandoori trout.

The Tower

Museum of Scotland, Chambers St
☎0131/225 3003, 🌐www.tower
-restaurant.com. Expensive but
excellent modern Scottish food,
such as shellfish and expensive
chargrilled Aberdeen Angus
steaks, in a self-consciously
chic setting on Level 5 of the
Museum of Scotland. At night
you're escorted along the empty
corridors to the restaurant,
where spectacular views to the
floodlit Castle are revealed.

Pubs and bars

Assembly

41 Lothian St ☎0131/220 4288,
🌐www.assemblybar.co.uk. Mon–Sun
9am–1am. This hip hangout is a
café-bar from breakfast through
to mid-afternoon, then revs up
in the evenings as a lively pre-
club venue, with a roster of DJs
through the week.

Blue Blazer

2 Spittal St ☎0131/229 5030. Daily 11am–1am. This traditional Edinburgh pub with an oak-clad bar and church pews serves as good a selection of real ales as you'll find anywhere in the city.

Bow Bar

80 The West Bow (Victoria St) ☎0131/226 7667. Daily 11am–11pm. Wonderful old wood-panelled bar that won an award as the best drinkers' pub in Britain a few years back. Choose from among nearly 150 whiskies, or a changing selection of first-rate Scottish and English cask beers.

Greyfriars Bobby Bar

34 Candlemaker Row ☎0131/225 8328. Daily 11am–1am. Slightly nondescript but long-established place named after the statue outside. It's popular with tourists as a result, but cheap bar food and its location close to the university make it a student haunt, too.

The Last Drop Tavern

74–78 Grassmarket ☎0131/225 4851. Daily 11am–1am. The "Drop" refers to the Edinburgh gallows, which were located out front, and whose former presence is symbolized in the red paintwork of the exterior. Serves cheapish pub food and, like its competitors in the same block, enjoys the patronage of students and stag and hen parties.

Traverse Bar Café

Traverse Theatre, 10 Cambridge St ☎0131/228 5383. Sun–Wed 11am–midnight, Thurs–Sat 11am–1am. Much more than just a theatre bar, attracting a lively, sophisticated crowd who dispel any notion of a quiet interval drink. Good food and snacks available after shows. One of *the* places to be during the Festival.

Villager

49–50 George IV Bridge. Daily 11am–1am. The bar of the moment in this part of town, so expect the local glitterati and lots of designer clothing in amongst the chocolate brown sofas and teetering bar stools.

PLACES South of the Royal Mile

▼ASSEMBLY BAR

Along Princes Street

Princes Street is very much the centre of Edinburgh, with trains pulling into Waverley Station, buses and taxis arriving from all points and the pavements thick with tourists and shoppers. The latter are found in their droves along the north side of the street, where chain stores and a hotch-potch of architectural styles create an unlovely prospect. This is immediately redeemed to the south via a swathe of gardens as well as monuments, grand galleries and an unforgettable vista of the castle and Old Town.

General Register House and New Register House

Princes St ☎0131/535 1314, ⓦwww
.nas.gov.uk. Mon–Fri 9am–4.45pm.
Free. With its dignified
Corinthian pillars and dome,
General Register House is the
most distinguished building
on Princes Street. It's best
seen on the approach from
North Bridge – the same
perspective is hard to achieve
closer up, which is why the
streams of shoppers squeezing
past routinely ignore it. It was
designed in 1774 by Robert
Adam as a custom-built home
for Scotland's historic records, a
function it has maintained ever
since, today acting as the home
for the National Archives of
Scotland. Its elegant interior is
centred on a glorious Roman
rotunda, lavishly decorated with
plasterwork and antique-style
medallions. Visitors can look
around the small exhibitions
based on the archives which are
mounted in the foyer, and while
access to other parts of the
building, including the rotunda,
is normally restricted to those
conducting historical research,
staff may allow you in if you
enquire at reception. Searches
into family history are normally
best begun at the adjacent New
Register House. This is the
home of the **General Register
Office** for Scotland (ⓦwww
.gro-scotland.gov.uk) and
contains records of births, deaths
and marriages. A dedicated
Scottish Family History Centre,
which will act as a single point

▲PRINCES STREET AT NIGHT

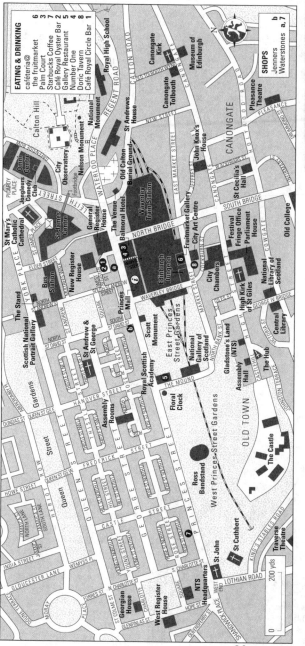

EATING & DRINKING
cáfeteria@ 6
the fruitmarket 3
Palm Court 7
Starbucks Coffee 2
Café Royal Oyster Bar 5
Gallery Restaurant 4
Number One 9
Doric Tavern 8
Café Royal Circle Bar 1

SHOPS
Jenners b
Waterstones a, 7

© Crown copyright

of access for those researching genealogical records, is due to open within General Register House in 2006.

Balmoral Hotel

1 Princes St ☎0131/556 2414, ⓦwww.thebalmoralhotel.com. Dominating the east end of Princes Street, the *Balmoral* was built as a railway hotel in the early 1900s. For much of the century it was known as the *North British Hotel*, though by the 1980s the use of the imperial "North Britain" as an alternative name for Scotland didn't impress too many locals. The 188-room, five-star establishment is one of the grandest hotels in the city, though it maintains its close association with the railway: the timepiece on its

▼BALMORAL HOTEL CLOCK

chunky clocktower always kept two minutes fast in order to encourage passengers to catch their trains at neighbouring Waverley Station, the city's principal mainline stop. Downstairs in the hotel is a Michelin-starred restaurant, *Number One* (see p.109); a meal in *Hadrian's Brasserie* or tea at the *Palm Court* (see p.108) is a more affordable way to get a taste of the place.

Edinburgh Dungeon

31 Market St ☎0131/240 1000, ⓦwww.thedungeons.com. Nov–March Mon–Fri 11am–4pm, Sat & Sun 10.30am–9.30pm; April–Jun daily 10am–5pm; July–Aug daily 10am–7pm; Sept–Oct daily 10am–5pm. £9.95. An unashamedly OTT horror-themed attraction which aptly describes itself as "an orgy of grisly entertainment", the Dungeon is based in vaults beside the railway station. If you're tempted inside by the blood-spattered marketing, you'll encounter various scenes that use actors and gruesome special effects to ham up Edinburgh's associations with blood and gore of all varieties, from sixteenth-century witchhunts to the bodysnatchers Burke and Hare. This isn't the place for historical authenticity, but it does do its best to scare the living daylights out of you.

Fruitmarket Gallery

45 Market St ☎0131/225 2383, ⓦwww.fruitmarket.co.uk. Mon–Sat 11am–5.30pm, Sun noon–5pm. Free. Much altered from its days as the city's fruit and veg market, the stylish modern design of this dynamic and much-admired art space is complemented by the regular appearance of top-grade international artists – recent years have seen shows by the

▲CITY ART CENTRE

likes of Jeff Koons and Bill Viola. With exhibitions changing every couple of months, this is one of the city's best places to see contemporary art. Peter Fink's exterior light installation, which mimics the Northern Lights, gives the building some interesting hues after dark; there's also a pleasant café and good art bookshop inside.

City Art Centre

2 Market St ☎ 0131/529 3993, ⊛ www .cac.org.uk. Mon–Sat 10am–5pm, plus Sun noon–5pm in July & Aug only. Free. This classic six-storey Old Town building is used by the city council to exhibit the best of their own impressive collection of Scottish art, as well as high-profile touring exhibitions. There's no permanent display, and shows can range from high-brow overviews of the history of Scottish art to props from *Star Wars*, but the larger exhibitions are normally worth checking out.

Princes Street Gardens

Princes St. Daily dawn–dusk. Free. It's hard to imagine that the gardens which flank nearly the entire length of Princes Street were once the stagnant, foul-smelling Nor' Loch, into which the effluent of the Old Town flowed for centuries. Initially, a canal was proposed to run through the gardens; the railways came along just in time to claim the space, and today a sunken cutting carries the main lines out of Waverley Station to the west and north. Once completed, the gardens, split into East and West sections, were the private domain of Princes Street residents and their well-placed acquaintances, only becoming a public park in 1876. These days, the swathes of green lawn, colourful flower beds and mature trees are a green lung for the city centre: local office workers appear in their droves on sunny days to take a picnic lunch, while others use it as a traffic-free short-cut. The gardens' eastern section is home to an ice rink (late Nov to early Jan daily 10am–10pm; £6.50) and a towering Ferris wheel (same times; £2) in the run-up to Christmas. The larger and more verdant western section holds a floral clock and the Ross Bandstand, a popular Festival venue.

Scott Monument

East Princes Street Gardens ☎0131/529 7902, ⊛www.cac.org.uk. Daily: April–Sept Mon–Sat 9am–6pm, Sun 10am–6pm; Oct–March Mon–Sat 9am–3pm, Sun 10am–3pm. £2.50. The most bizarre of Princes Street's assorted sights, and the largest memorial to a man of letters anywhere in the world, the 200ft-high Scott Monument was erected in memory of prolific author and patriot Sir Walter Scott within a few years of his death in 1832. Regarded as the father of the modern novel, Scott was born in Edinburgh in 1771 and studied law at the University, gaining fame initially for resurrecting old Scottish folklore and ballads. Though originally published anonymously, his famous *Waverley* novels made him a celebrity, and by the 1820s he was playing a central role in Scottish affairs, famously coordinating George IV's visit to Edinburgh and dressing the king up in tartan. The elaborate Gothic space rocket which commemorates Scott was designed by one George Meikle Kemp, a local carpenter and joiner; while it was still under construction, he stumbled into a canal one foggy evening and drowned. The architecture is closely modelled on Scott's beloved Melrose Abbey, while the rich sculptural decoration shows 64 characters from his novels. On the central plinth at the base of the monument is a statue of the writer with his deerhound Maida, carved from a thirty-ton block of Carrara marble. Inside the recently restored memorial, a tightly winding spiral staircase climbs to a narrow platform near the top: from here, you can enjoy some inspiring – if vertiginous – vistas of the city below and hills and firths beyond.

National Gallery of Scotland

The Mound ☎0131/624 6200, ⊛www .natgalscot.ac.uk. Daily Mon–Sun 10am–5pm, plus Thurs till 7pm. Free, though some temporary exhibitions carry an entrance charge. Scotland's national collection of historic international art centres on the two Neoclassical temples which sit alongside each other at the foot of the Mound.

▼CLASSICAL STATUES, NATIONAL GALLERY OF SCOTLAND

The original National Gallery building, furthest from Princes Street, was designed by William Playfair in the 1850s to echo but not mimic its earlier and more exuberant neighbour, the Royal Scottish Academy (see below). The National Gallery has its own entrance, but the Weston Link, built beneath the RSA and with a prominent entry point from East Princes Street Gardens, allows access to all parts of the gallery. Contained within the National Gallery building is Scotland's premier collection of pre-twentieth-century European art, including a clutch of exquisite Old Masters and some superb Impressionist works. Though by no means as vast as national collections found elsewhere in Europe, the gallery benefits greatly from being a manageable size, its series of elegant octagonal rooms enlivened by imaginative displays and a pleasantly unrushed atmosphere. The innovative and often controversial influence of the its flamboyant director, Timothy Clifford, is immediately apparent on the ground floor, where the rooms have been restored to their 1850s appearance with pictures hung closely together on claret-coloured walls, often on two levels, and intermingled with sculptures and *objets d'art* to produce a deliberately cluttered effect. As a result some lesser works, which would otherwise languish in the vaults, are displayed a good fifteen feet up. Though individual works are frequently rearranged, the layout is broadly chronological, starting in the upper rooms above the entrance, and continuing clockwise around the ground floor. Not all of the finest pieces are guaranteed to be on show, but it's worth looking out for highlights such as a superbly restored Botticelli, *The Virgin Adoring the Sleeping Christ Child*, as well as various important canvases by Titian and other Venetians, a poignant Rembrandt self-portrait, a rare Vermeer titled *Christ in the House of Martha and Mary*, and the excellent range of early, classic and post-Impressionist works, including some Degas bronzes and works by Gauguin, Van Gogh and Cézanne. Amongst the Scottish collection in the basement, there's a great introduction to the portraiture skills of Sir Henry Raeburn; his "skating minister" (which inspired Enric Miralles' designs for the new Scottish Parliament) is probably the gallery's best-loved piece.

Royal Scottish Academy

The Mound ☎0131/225 6671, @www.royalscottishacademy.org. Daily Mon–Sun 10am–5pm, Thurs till 7pm. Free. The elder and more extravagant of the two buildings which form the National Gallery of Scotland (see p.106) houses the Royal Scottish Academy, a private institution made up of the country's finest artists and architects. The annual RSA

The National Galleries of Scotland

The National Gallery of Scotland is just one part of Edinburgh's national art collections. Elsewhere in the city, the Scottish National Portrait Gallery (see p.110), the Scottish National Gallery of Modern Art (p.128) and its neighbour the Dean Gallery (p.130) display other parts of the National Galleries' holdings. A free bus service (Mon–Sat 11am–5pm, Sun noon–5pm) connects all four buildings.

exhibition (April & May) is regarded as Scotland's pre-eminent show of work by living artists, while at other times of the year the twelve recently refurbished interior rooms over two levels are hung with major temporary exhibitions mounted by the National Gallery – recent highlights have been shows based on Monet and Titian. Designed by William Playfair in 1826 and extended by the same architect in 1836, the building displays a profusion of Neoclassical columns and detail, including a guard of sphinxes on the roof alongside a statue of Queen Victoria. The plaza outside is a popular spot for buskers, stalls and impromptu Fringe performances.

Shops

Jenners

48 Princes St ☏0131/225 2442, ⊛www.jenners.com. Edinburgh's oldest department store and often dubbed "the Harrods of the North", the venerable Jenners dates from the late nineteenth century and remains the retail experience of choice for Morningside ladies and New Town gentry. Still a few hints of *Are You Being Served?*, though modern designer labels now set the tone.

Waterstone's

13–14 Princes St ☏0131/556 3034. As Edinburgh's independent booksellers have largely been squeezed out of business, it's the national chains which dominate. This one gives proper prominence to local guidebooks and Scottish writers, as well as hosting regular readings and events.

Cafés

Fruitmarket Gallery Café

Fruitmarket Gallery, 45 Market St ☏0131/226 1843, ⊛www.fruitmarket .co.uk/cafe.html. This attractive café feels like an extension of the gallery space, its airy, reflective ambience enhanced by the wall of glass onto the street. Stop in for soups, coffees or a caesar salad.

Palm Court

Balmoral Hotel, 1 Princes St ☏0131/556 2414. A smart suite within the five-star *Balmoral*,

▼ALLAN RAMSAY STATUE, PRINCES STREET

where elevenses, pre-prandial nibbles or proper afternoon teas with scones or egg-and-cress sandwiches are served to the melodic sounds of a harpist.

Starbucks Coffee

Waterstone's, 128 Princes St ☎0131/226 3610. One chain coffee shop worth mentioning, surrounded by books and with fantastic views across Princes Street Gardens to the castle.

Restaurants

Café Royal Oyster Bar

17a West Register St ☎0131/556 4124. An Edinburgh classic, with a splendidly ornate Victorian interior featuring stained-glass windows, marble floors and Doulton tiling. The expensive seafood dishes, including freshly caught oysters, are served in a civilized, chatty setting.

Gallery Restaurant

Weston Link, National Gallery for Scotland ☎0131/624 6580. Closed Sun eve. Swish dining option in the new extension below the National Gallery, offering expensive modern Scottish dishes such as scallops with black pudding or Aberdeen Angus fillet with smoked garlic. Large glass windows offer views of Princes Street Gardens; it's busy by day but takes on a more detached feel in the evenings once the galleries have closed.

Number One

1 Princes St ☎0131/557 6727, ⓦwww .thebalmoralhotel.com/restaurant1 .html. Closed Sat & Sun lunch. Chef Jeff Bland has recently scored a Michelin star for his haute cuisine served in an overtly upmarket subterranean dining space. Lunches are (just about) affordable for a taste of the artistry; for a bravura performance there's a six-course tasting menu, with dishes such as foie gras poached in port, for £55.

Doric Tavern

15–16 Market St ☎0131/225 1084, ⓦwww.thedoric.co.uk. Long-established, unpretentious bistro overlooking Waverley Station; the moderately priced food tends towards the predictable end of modern Scottish cooking, with the likes of lamb cutlets served with onion marmalade, but it's a popular, easy-going spot with a pleasant wine bar alongside the dining room.

Pubs and bars

Café Royal Circle Bar

19 West Register St ☎0131/556 1884. Mon–Wed 11am–11pm, Fri & Sat 11am–1am, Sun 12.30–10pm. As memorable as the *Oyster Bar* next door, the *Café Royal* is worth a visit just for its Victorian decor, notably the huge elliptical island bar and the tiled portraits of renowned inventors. More than that, the beer and food are good, too.

▼MARKET STREET PUB

The New Town

From its outset, the New Town was planned as a total contrast to the Old Town: the layout was to be symmetrical, the streets broad and straight, and the architecture unashamedly grand and spacious. Though originally intended as a residential area, the central part of the New Town is now the bustling hub of the city's professional and business life, dominated by shops, banks and offices. Its unique historic character, however, is obvious at every turn, especially if you head for the dignified Georgian streets to the north, which remain one of the best-planned, elegant quarters of any European city.

Scottish National Portrait Gallery

1 Queen St ☎0131/624 6200, ⊛www
.natgalscot.ac.uk. Daily 10am–5pm,
plus Thurs till 7pm. Free, entrance
charge for some temporary exhibitions.
A fantastic medieval Gothic palace in red sandstone, the Portrait Gallery makes an extravagant contrast to the New Town's prevailing Neoclassicism. The exterior of the building is encrusted with statues of famous national heroes, a theme reiterated in the stunning two-storey entrance hall by William Hole's tapestry-like frieze depicting notable figures from Scotland's past. Unlike the more global outlook of its sister National Galleries (see pp.106–7), the portrait gallery devotes itself to images of famous Scots – a definition stretched to include anyone with the slightest connection to the country. Taken as a whole, it's an engaging procession through Scottish history, with familiar faces from Bonnie Prince Charlie and Mary, Queen of Scots, to Alex Ferguson and

The design of the New Town

Various schemes for the expansion of Edinburgh to the land north of the Old Town were suggested through the eighteenth century, but it wasn't until 1766 that a competition to design the New Town was held, and eventually won by 22-year-old local lad James Craig. His initial plan was based on the pattern of the Union Jack flag; the modified final version kept the Unionist street names but simplified the layout. The principal axis, George Street, was to run along the brow of the hill linking two elegant squares; parallel Queen Street and Princes Street would have houses on one side only, looking north to the Forth and south to the castle respectively. Interlinking streets were to run at right angles to the main thoroughfares, creating neat blocks of houses, with narrow lanes providing access for tradesmen and carriages. Once implemented, the design proved to be the finest example of classical town planning in Europe, the geometric pattern of streets subsequently copied not just in Glasgow during the nineteenth century, but also in many expanding North American cities such as New York and Chicago. The importance of Edinburgh's legacy was recognised in the 1990s when the New Town (in combination with the Old Town) was designed a World Heritage Site by UNESCO.

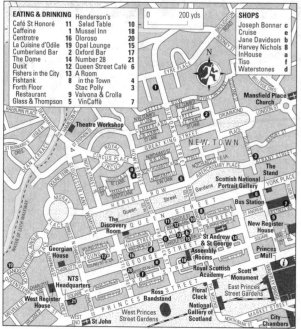

EATING & DRINKING		
Café St Honoré	11	
Caffeine	1	
Centrotre	16	
La Cuisine d'Odile	19	
Cumberland Bar	2	
The Dome	14	
Dusit	12	
Fishers in the City		
Fishtank	8	
Forth Floor		
Restaurant	9	
Glass & Thompson	5	
Henderson's		
Salad Table	10	
Mussel Inn	18	
Oloroso	20	
Opal Lounge	15	
Oxford Bar	17	
Number 28	21	
Queen Street Café	6	
A Room		
in the Town	4	
Stac Polly	3	
Valvona & Crolla	13	
VinCaffè	7	

SHOPS	
Joseph Bonnar	c
Cruise	e
Jane Davidson	b
Harvey Nichols	8
InHouse	a
Tiso	f
Waterstones	d

© Crown copyright

Sean Connery appearing along the way. The permanent collection is located on the

▼SCOTTISH NATIONAL PORTRAIT GALLERY

two upper floors; though the paintings on display are changed frequently, there's normally a healthy representation of works by Scotland's best portraitists, from Allan Ramsay and Sir Henry Raeburn to contemporary luminaries such as David Mach and John Bellany. Temporary exhibitions are displayed in the galleries on the ground floor; elsewhere on this floor are the shop and café.

The Discovery Room

52 Queen St ☎0131/225 6028. Mon–Fri 9am–5pm. Free, but donation requested. This underplayed but highly significant spot is where Edinburgh doctor Sir James Young Simpson discovered the anaesthetic applications of chloroform, which revolutionized medicine in the mid-nineteenth century

PLACES

The New Town

The colonization of Princes Street, George Street and Queen Street by shops and offices means that it can be hard to appreciate the elegant residential style which made the first phase of the New Town so attractive to Edinburgh's middle and upper classes in the late eighteenth century. Take a stroll down the hill to the later phases of the New Town and you'll find yourself in purely residential territory. Although many of the townhouses are now subdivided into flats, distinctive period features remain intact, including the fan-shaped windows above heavy doors with brass name plaques and handles, the stone detailing and tall, astragaled windows. Few streets fail to impress in what is, after all, a World Heritage Site, but to see some of the finest examples, walk the short circuit from Heriot Row through to Moray Place, along Doune Terrace and Gloucester Place then back up India Street.

by providing the first effective form of pain relief in childbirth. The townhouse where Simpson lived and had his practice rooms is now run by the Church of Scotland as a drug counselling centre, but the old dining room where he made his first public demonstration of chloroform at a dinner party in 1847 has been left as a museum, with story-boards about Simpson's career and his experiments with different anaesthetics lining the walls, and books and pamphlets set out on a central table. Though a little dowdy in appearance and inevitably of most appeal to those with an interest in medical history, the Discovery Room has an appealing simplicity and authenticity, and covers its subject as equally effectively as more glamorous history-themed museums.

Charlotte Square

Marking the western end of George Street, Charlotte Square is generally regarded as the epitome of the New Town's elegant simplicity. Designed by Robert Adam in 1791, it immediately became the most exclusive residential address in Edinburgh, and though

much of it is now occupied by offices, the imperious dignity of the architecture is still clear to see. Indeed, the north side, the finest of Adam's drawings, is once again the city's premier address, with the official residence of the First Minister of the Scottish Parliament at number 6 (Bute House), the

▼CHARLOTTE SQUARE

▲MORAY PLACE

Edinburgh equivalent of 10 Downing Street. In August each year, the gardens in the centre of the square are colonized by the temporary tents of the Edinburgh Book Festival (see p.178).

The Georgian House

7 Charlotte Square ☎0131/225 2160, ⓦwww.nts.org.uk. Daily: March & Nov–Dec 11am–3pm; April–Oct 10am–5pm. £5. As the National Trust for Scotland's Gladstone's Land (see p.71) represents classic Old Town life, so their Georgian House provides a revealing sense of well-to-do New Town living in the early nineteenth century. Though a little stuffy and lifeless, the rooms are impressively decked out in period furniture – look for the working barrel organ which plays a selection of Scottish airs – and hung with fine paintings, including portraits by Ramsay and Raeburn, seventeenth-century Dutch cabinet pictures, and the beautiful *Marriage of the Virgin* by El Greco's teacher, the Italian miniaturist Giulio Clovio. In the basement are the original wine cellar, lined with roughly

made bins, and a kitchen complete with an open fire for roasting and a separate oven for baking; video reconstructions of life below and above stairs are shown in a nearby room.

National Trust for Scotland Headquarters

28 Charlotte Square ☎0131/243 9300, ⓦwww.nts.org.uk. Mon–Sat 9.30am–4.30pm. Free. The NTS's love affair with Charlotte Square is continued on the south side, most of which is taken up with their headquarters. The buildings have been superbly restored over the past few years to something approaching their Georgian grandeur, and it's well worth taking a look at the sumptuous interior with its wooden panelling, intricate cornicing and large, bright rooms. On the first floor, a small gallery (Mon–Fri 11am–3pm; free) shows a collection of twentieth-century Scottish art, including a number of attractive examples of the work of the Scottish Colourists, while two adjoining rooms offer an introduction to the Trust in general, with a video showing highlights of their properties around Scotland. Downstairs, there's a café (see p.116) and a shop selling National Trust books and souvenirs.

Dundas Street

Dundas St. A steeply inclined extension of Hanover Street, Dundas Street has a fantastic concentration of commercial art galleries which make for excellent browsing. While all are relatively small compared with Edinburgh's large public galleries, casual viewing is positively encouraged here and the work shown is almost always for sale, with prices ranging from a few hundred pounds for

▲DUNDAS STREET GALLERIES

a limited-edition print to tens of thousands for work by the best-known contemporary artists from around the UK. Changing exhibitions give a different slant to each of the galleries listed below, though most places will show work by more than one artist at any given time. The very best of the bunch are right at the top of the street, on the corner of Abercromby Place: the dynamic Open Eye Gallery (Mon–Fri 10am–6pm, Sat 10am–4pm; ☎0131/557 1020, ⓦwww.openeyegallery.co.uk) features a number of Scotland's top contemporary artists. Other worthwhile stops nearby are Phoenix 369 at no. 3 (Tues–Sat noon–6pm, ☎0131/556 6497), which majors in international contemporary work; the grander Bourne Fine Art at no. 6 (Mon–Fri 10am–6pm, Sat 11am–2pm; ☎0131/557 4050,ⓦwww .bournefineart.com), which specializes in Scottish art from 1700–1950; and, at no.16, the spacious Scottish Gallery (Mon–Fri 10am–6pm, Sat

10am–4pm; ☎0131/558 1200, ⓦwww.scottish-gallery.co.uk), the oldest private gallery in Scotland, with a basement area dedicated to applied art. Further down are a number of smaller venues alongside antique and secondhand shops – the Torrance Gallery at no.36 (Mon–Fri 11am–6pm, Sat 10.30am–4pm; ☎0131/556 6366, ⓦwww.torrancegallery .co.uk), one of the first galleries in Edinburgh to specialize in contemporary art; and the Randolph Gallery at no.39 (Mon–Fri 10.30am–6pm, Sat 10am–4pm; ☎0131/556 0808, ⓦwww.randolphgallery.com), which tends to show a varied range of local art and crafts.

Shops

Joseph Bonnar

72 Thistle St ☎0131/226 2811. Closed Sun. This wonderfully old-fashioned shop, with its dazzling range of antique gems and trinkets, is the most intriguing

of Thistle Street's string of jewellers.

Cruise

80 George St ☎0131/226 3524. A home-grown name which is highly rated by the Edinburgh's fashionistas. Of the number of outlets around town, the big George Street branch has all the latest in cool men's designer clothes.

Jane Davidson

52 Thistle St ☎0131/225 3280, ⊛www.janedavidson.com. Closed Sun. A discreet frontage to three floors of the hautest of couture for women. Much loved by Edinburgh ladies who find department stores distasteful and have access to a shimmering credit card.

Harvey Nichols

30–34 St Andrew Square ☎0131/524 8388, ⊛www.harveynichols.com. Edinburgh's style cats were greatly relieved when Harvey Nicks finally arrived in town, offering three floors of expensive designer labels and an impressive food hall and restaurant.

InHouse

28 Howe St ☎0131/225 2888 ⊛www.inhousenet.co.uk. Closed Sun. Covetable contemporary furniture, lighting and kitchenware from designers including Flos, Cassina and Alessi.

Tiso

123–125 Rose St ☎0131/225 9486, ⊛www.tiso.com. Thurs till 7.30pm. The city centre's widest selection of good-quality outdoor gear, with waterproof jackets, boots and camping and sporting gadgets.

Cafés

Caffeine

154 Dundas St; no phone. Closed Sat & Sun. A simple, contemporary coffee bar, owned and run by locals who pride themselves on knowing a thing or two about brewing the black stuff. As the clientele are mostly office workers, it closes by mid-afternoon.

▼CRUISE, GEORGE STREET

▲CAFÉ ST HONORÉ

Glass & Thompson

2 Dundas St ☎0131/557 0909.
Tasteful, upmarket café-deli
with huge bowls of olives and
an irresistible glass counter filled
with lovely food; scattered tables
and chairs mean you can linger
over a made-to-order sandwich
or top-notch cake and coffee.

Number 28

NTS Headquarters, 28 Charlotte
Square ☎0131/243 9339. Closed
Sun. Refined café authentically
decked out with severe
Georgian family portraits,
serving porridge with cream for
breakfast, classy light lunches
and daytime tea and scones.

Queen Street Café

Scottish National Portrait Gallery, 1
Queen St ☎0131/557 2844. Tucked
away from the main galleries,
this self-service café enjoys a
pleasantly unhurried atmosphere,
and specializes in homemade
soups, quiches and sweet treats.

Restaurants

Café St Honoré

34 North West Thistle St Lane
☎0131/226 2211, ⊛www
.cafesthonore.com. A little piece
of Paris discreetly tucked away
in a New Town back lane.
Fairly traditional French fare
– grilled oysters, warm duck
salad and tarte tatin – but top
quality at moderate prices.

Centrotre

103 George St ☎0131/225 1550,
⊛www.centotre.com. Closed Sun.
Slick but welcoming bar, café
and restaurant in an ornate
former bank, offering unfussy,
top-quality Italian food from
fresh pastries and coffee to
interesting pizzas or a simple
but blissful plate of gorgonzola
served with a ripe pear. All
accompanied by a seriously
impressive drinks list.

La Cuisine d'Odile

Institut Français d'Ecosse, 13
Randolph Crescent ☎0131/225 5685.
Closed Sun, Mon & July. Genuine
lunch-only French home
cooking in a basement under
the French Institute. There's
a really authentic feel to the
food, with lots of inexpensive
terrines, flans, game dishes and
some superb desserts, including
a signature "Choc'Odile"
chocolate tart.

Dusit

49a Thistle St ☏0131/220 6846, ⊛www.dusit.co.uk. The bold but effective blend of Thai flavours and well-sourced Scottish ingredients here brings a bit of originality and refinement to the often-predictable Thai dining scene. The moderately priced specialities include guinea fowl with red curry sauce or vegetables stir-fried with a dash of whisky.

Fishers in the City

58 Thistle St ☏1031/225 5109, ⊛www.fishersbistros.co.uk. The New Town incarnation of Leith's best-loved seafood bistro has a sleek modern interior, great service and some stunning (if expensive) seafood such as cod with black olive tapenade, or whole grilled lemon sole.

Forth Floor Restaurant

Harvey Nichols, 30–34 St Andrew Square ☏0131/524 8350, ⊛www .harveynichols.com. Closed Sun, Mon evening. Another Edinburgh restaurant with a view, and showing real confidence in its fine modern Scottish options

– seared scallops with fig salsa, perhaps, or pot-roast pork. The expensive restaurant gets the glass frontage; the brasserie, with its simpler risottos and grills, is less pricey but set back from the views.

Henderson's Salad Table

94 Hanover St ☏0131/225 2131, ⊛www.hendersonsofedinburgh. co.uk. Closed Sun. A much-loved Edinburgh institution, this self-service basement vegetarian restaurant offers freshly prepared hot dishes plus a decent choice of salads, soups and cakes. The slightly antiquated cafeteria feel can be off-putting, but the food is honest, reliable and always tasty. Light live jazz every evening.

Mussel Inn

61–65 Rose St ☏0131/225 5979, ⊛www.mussel-inn.com. After feasting on a kilo of mussels and a basket of chips for under £10, you'll realize why there's a demand to get in here. The owners are west-coast shellfish farmers, which ensures that the time from sea to stomach is minimal.

▼WALL MOSAICS, MUSSEL INN

Oloroso

33 Castle St ☏0131/226 7614, ⊛www .oloroso.co.uk. Edinburgh's most glamorous upmarket dining space, with a rooftop location giving views to the Castle and the Forth. The expensive menu features strong flavours

such as chump of lamb or roast salmon, followed by playful puddings –try the deep-fried jam sandwich with ice cream. Eating (or drinking) from the less intense bar is the cost-effective way to enjoy the setting, but the best views are from the balcony.

A Room in the Town

18 Howe St ☎0131/225 8204, ⊛www .aroomin.co.uk/thetown. Manages to combine a homely, relaxed atmosphere with decent, Scottish-slanted seasonal food. You can bring your own alcohol, which keeps the bills down.

Stac Polly

29–33 Dublin St ☎0131/556 2231. Closed lunchtimes Sat & Sun. Teetering on the edge of overbearing Scottishness, *Stac Polly* avoids the kitsch with some classy touches, atmospheric surroundings and a hearty menu of game, fish and meat dishes.

Pubs and bars

Cumberland Bar

1–3 Cumberland St ☎0131/558 3134. Mon–Sat 11am–1am, Sun 12.30–11pm. One of the few pubs in this part of the New Town, this mellow, cultured, old-fashioned place full of wood panelling and cosy nooks is a delightful find, and serves excellent cask-conditioned ales.

The Dome

14 George St ☎0131/624 8624. Mon–Sat 11am–1am, Sun 12.30–11pm. Opulent conversion of a massive George Street bank, thronging with well-dressed locals. Probably the most impressive bar interior in the city, with Grecian columns and a huge glass dome, while the stylish cocktail bar at the side is reminiscent of a 1920s cruise ship.

Fishtank

16a Queen St ☎0131/226 5959. Mon–Sat 4pm–1am, Sun 6pm–1am. A refreshing alternative in the New Town, where brashest is often best, this is a tiny subterranean bar where fish provide the animated decoration and the prevailing vibe is friendly and chilled-out.

Opal Lounge

51a George St ☎0131/226 2275. Daily noon–3am. A low-ceilinged bar with a faintly Oriental theme, loud music and a long cocktail list. Over-dressed twentysomethings flock in for a glimpse of local celebrities or Prince William, but usually have to stand in a queue and squeeze past the bouncers to get in.

Oxford Bar

8 Young St ☎0131/226 2275. Mon–Sun noon–3am. An unpretentious, unspoilt, no-nonsense city bar – which is why local crime writer Ian Rankin and his Inspector Rebus like it so much. Fans duly make the pilgrimage, but fortunately not all the regulars have been scared off.

Valvona & Crolla VinCaffè

11 Multrees Walk ☎0131/557 0088, wwww.valvonacrolla.com. Suave, Milanese-style venue, with a stand-up espresso bar and takeaway downstairs, and snacks, meals and fifty delicious wines by the glass upstairs.

Calton Hill and Broughton

Edinburgh's longstanding tag as the "Athens of the North" is nowhere better earned than on Calton Hill, the volcanic crag which rises up above the eastern end of Princes Street. Numerous architects homed in on it as a showcase for their most ambitious and grandiose buildings and monuments, whose presence emphasize Calton's aloof air and sense of detachment today. But the hill and its odd collection of buildings aren't just for looking at: this is also one of the best viewpoints from which to appreciate the city as a whole, with its tightly knitted suburbs, landmark Old and New Town buildings and, beyond, the sea, which is much closer to Edinburgh than many visitors expect.

Calton Old Burial Ground

Waterloo Place. Open during daylight hours. Free. Before the building of Waterloo Place and Regent Bridge (the elevated roadway which extends eastwards from Princes Street), Calton Hill was separated from both the Old and New Towns by steep-sided valleys. The hill was formerly the site of a jail (demolished

▼ADAM SMITH MEMORIAL, CALTON OLD BURIAL GROUND

in the 1930s to make way for the looming Art Deco St Andrew's House, occupied by civil servants) and Calton Old graveyard, which survives today tucked in behind a line of high, dark, forbidding walls. The picturesque assembly of mausoleums and gravestones within, some at a jaunty angle and others weathered with age, make for an absorbing wander. Notable among the monuments is the cylindrical memorial by Robert Adam to the philosopher David Hume, one of Edinburgh's greatest sons, and a piercing obelisk commemorating various political martyrs.

Old Royal High School

Regent Road. No public access. With its bold central portico of Doric columns and graceful symmetrical colonnaded wings, Thomas Hamilton's elegant building of 1829 is regarded by many as the epitome of Edinburgh's Athenian aspirations. The capital's high

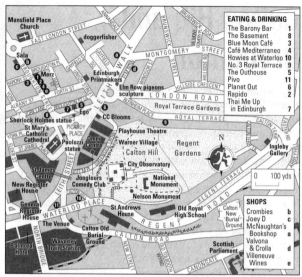

EATING & DRINKING

The Barony Bar	1
The Basement	8
Blue Moon Café	3
Café Mediterraneo	4
Howies at Waterloo	10
No. 3 Royal Terrace	9
The Outhouse	5
Pivo	11
Planet Out	6
Rapido	2
Thai Me Up in Edinburgh	7

SHOPS

Crombies	b
Joey D	c
McNaughtan's Bookshop	a
Valvona & Crolla	d
Villeneuve Wines	e

school was based here between 1829 and 1968, at which point the building was converted to house a debating chamber and became Scotland's parliament-in-waiting. However after the 1997 referendum, which came out in support of the re-establishment of a Scottish parliament, the building was controversially rejected as too small for the intended assembly, with a brand-new building at Holyrood favoured instead.

Currently used as offices by the city council, the latest plan is to convert it into a museum of the history of photography, based around the work of 1840s photographic pioneers David Octavius Hill and Robert Adamson, whose studio, Rock House, was located on Calton Hill below the Observatory.

Ingleby Gallery

6 Carlton Terrace ☎0131/556 4441, ⊛www.inglebygallery.com. Tues–Sat

▼OLD ROYAL HIGH SCHOOL

10am–5pm. Free. The loop of terraced streets which run around the eastern side of Calton Hill are among the finest examples of the New Town's Georgian grandeur. Most are still residential, although there are a number of diplomatic offices here, including the now heavily guarded USA Consulate. One typically elegant Edinburgh townhouse is occupied by the Ingleby Gallery, probably the most impressive small private art gallery in town, where you can view changing exhibitions by international contemporary artists including many of Scotland's premier stars such as Alison Watt, Craigie Aitchison and Callum Innes.

Nelson Monument

Calton Hill ⓉⒺ 0131/556 2716, Ⓦ www .cac.org.uk. April–Sept Mon 1–6pm, Tues–Sat 10am–6pm; Oct–March Mon–Sat 10am–3pm. £2. Unusual in both its shape (an upside-down telescope) and theme (the victor at Trafalgar, generally regarded as one of England's, rather than Scotland's, great heroes), the Nelson Monument holds a prominent position at the top of Calton Hill. If you're feeling fit and want to upgrade Calton Hill's already impressive city views, you can climb the 143-step spiral staircase inside the monument; at the top, a viewing deck provides an interesting bird's-eye view of the odd assortment of buildings immediately alongside. Each day at 1pm, a white ball drops down a mast at the top of the monument; this, together with the one o'clock gun fired from the Castle battlements (see p.69), once provided a daily check for the mariners of Leith, who needed accurate chronometers to ensure reliable navigation at sea.

National Monument

Calton Hill. Although it's often referred to as "Edinburgh's Disgrace", many locals admire this unfinished and somewhat ungainly attempt to replicate the Parthenon atop Calton Hill. Begun as a memorial to the dead of the Napoleonic Wars, a shortage of funds for the project led architect William Playfair to ensure that even with just twelve of the massive columns completed, the folly would still serve as a striking landmark. It's one of those constructions which is purposeless yet still magnetic; with a bit of effort and care you can climb up and around the monument, sit and stare for a while from one of the huge steps or play hide-and-seek around the base of the mighty pillars. New schemes for the development of the National Monument and its Calton Hill neighbours, either grandiose or foolish (or both), are regularly proposed – one of these may some day be carried out.

City Observatory

Calton Hill. Designed by Playfair in 1818, the City Observatory is the largest of the buildings at the summit of Calton Hill. Because of pollution and the advent of street lighting, which impaired views of the stars, the observatory proper had to be relocated to Blackford Hill before the end of the nineteenth century, but the equipment here continues to be used by students. At one corner of the curtain walls is the castellated Observatory House, one of the few surviving buildings by James Craig, designer of the New Town. The complex isn't open to the public, but a stroll around its perimeter does offer a broad

▲ SHERLOCK HOLMES STATUE, PICARDY PLACE

part sculpture by Edinburgh-born Sir Eduardo Paolozzi. Titled *Manuscript of Monte Cassino*, it includes a giant hand holding a pair of tiny copulating grasshoppers and a robotic foot often employed by local toddlers as a makeshift slide. On the north side of the roundabout, set in front of a line of Georgian townhouses, is a statue of Sherlock Holmes who, though better associated with Baker Street in London, is commemorated here in tribute to

perspective over the city, with views out to the Forth Bridges and Fife.

Picardy Place

Between Calton Hill and the Broughton area, the large roundabout of Picardy Place links Leith Walk with the southeast corner of the New Town. It suffers from a high volume of traffic and a mess of conflicting architectural styles, in particular the brown concrete oblongs of the St James Centre, regularly cited as Edinburgh's greatest architectural blunder, and the new Omni Centre, which tries to make up for, in plate glass, what it lacks in grace. In amongst all these, however, are a few intriguing discoveries. At the foot of the steps in front of St Mary's Roman Catholic Cathedral is a wonderful three-

his creator Sir Arthur Conan Doyle, who was born close by in 1869 and went on to study medicine at Edinburgh University, modelling his famous detective on one of his professors.

Broughton Street

Forming the eastern fringe of the New Town, Broughton Street is central Edinburgh's bohemian quarter, its string of bars, restaurants, food shops and arty boutiques making it a relaxed place to wander or hang out. It's also the centre of the city's gay scene, with a number of clubs, bars and gay-oriented organizations comfortably, rather than overtly, mixing into the general meld. While there aren't any mainstream tourist attractions hereabouts, the area does hold several contemporary art galleries. The best of these are Edinburgh Printmakers at 23 Union Street (Tues–Sat 10am–6pm; ☎0131/557 2479, ⊛www .edinburgh-printmakers .co.uk), which has a studio and gallery dedicated to contemporary printmaking; the small but sparse doggerfisher at 11 Gayfield Square (Wed–Fri 11am–6pm, Sat noon–5pm; ☎0131/558 7110, ⊛www .doggerfisher.com), which shows avant-garde contemporary work in a converted tyre garage; and Merz at 87 Broughton Street (Wed–Sat noon–6pm, ☎0131/558 8778, ⊛www .merzart.com), where famous names (Tracey Emin, Iain Hamilton Finlay) are shown alongside high-quality work from less well known (and therefore less expensive) artists.

Mansfield Place Church

15 Mansfield Place ⊛www .mansfieldtraquair.org.uk. Normally open on the second Sun of every month, 1–4pm, plus Mon–Sat 10–11.45am in Aug. Free. Built in neo-Norman style between 1872 and 1885 by Sir Robert Rowand Anderson for the Catholic Apostolic Church, the interior of this lovingly restored building is dominated by an outstanding scheme of mural decorations by Dublin-born Arts and Crafts artist Phoebe Anna Traquair. Covering vast areas of the walls and ceilings of the main nave and side chapels, the wonderfully luminous paintings depict Biblical parables and texts, with rows of angels, cherubs flecked with gold and worshipping figures painted in delicate pastel colours. The dilapidation of the church by the early 1990s prompted a campaign to save and protect the murals, which are now recognized as the city's finest in-situ art treasure.

Shops

Crombies

97–101 Broughton St ☎0131/557 0111, ⊛www.sausages.co.uk. Closed Sun. Third-generation local butcher specializing in sausages, with over 100 different recipes: prune with cognac or basil,

PLACES Calton Hill and Broughton

▼PHOEBE ANNA TRAQUAIR MURALS, MANSFIELD PLACE CHURCH

beef and blackberries alongside the more familiar Cumberland, Toulouse and chipolatas.

Joey D

54 Broughton St ☎0131/557 6672, ⓦwww.d54industries.co.uk. Don't mistake this tiny place for a fusty secondhand clothes shop – instead you'll find innovative recycled fashion wear for men and women, all designed and made on the premises.

McNaughtan's Bookshop

3a–4a Haddington Place ☎0131/556 5897. Closed Sun & Mon. A fairly highbrow secondhand and antiquarian bookshop, with impressive sections on history, travel, art and Scottish classics.

Valvona & Crolla

19 Elm Row ☎0131/556 6066, ⓦwww.valvonacrolla.com. Arguably the finest Italian deli in Britain, with a van rolling in from Italy every week filled with the best possible produce. The floor-to-ceiling shelves are packed with wonderful cheeses, olive oils, salamis and wine, and a café at the back gives you the chance to indulge on the spot.

Villeneuve Wines

49a Broughton St ☎0131/558 8441, ⓦwww.villeneuvewines.com. Of Edinburgh's refreshing number of independent wine retailers, this has won crates of awards for their lively range of wines from small producers in both Old and New worlds. They also stock an impressive range of whiskies and Scottish beers.

Cafés

Café Mediterraneo

73 Broughton St ☎0131/557 6900. A friendly little place with a deli counter and a small dining space, serving inexpensive Italian-ish food in unpretentious style – not a red-checked table cloth to be seen. Open till 10pm Fri and Sat.

Blue Moon Café

1 Barony St ☎0131/557 0911. One of the best-known beacons of Edinburgh's gay scene, this easy-going, straight-friendly café-bar serves decent coffee, hearty breakfasts and moderately priced light meals right through to 11pm.

Restaurants

No. 3 Royal Terrace

3 Royal Terrace ☎0131/477 4747, ⓦwww.no3royalterrace.com. Pleasant if unadventurous mid-price dining on the ground floor of a grand Calton Hill townhouse – good for chargrilled steaks, fish and contemporary classics like Thai fishcakes or crème brûlée.

Howies at Waterloo

29 Waterloo Place ☎0131/556 5766, ⓦwww.howies.uk.com. Flagship of the Edinburgh-based mini-chain, with an elegant dining room close to Calton Hill's main sights and reliably well-priced, comforting modern

▼HOWIES AT WATERLOO

▲THE BASEMENT BAR

Scottish food such as salmon with an orange and vanilla butter sauce, or pigeon with caramelized apple.

Rapido

77–79 Broughton St ☎0131/556 2041. The best fish and chip shop in the area, and it even opens after the pubs and clubs spill out. If you don't fancy the deep-fried fare there are pizzas, bruschetta and takeaway pasta options.

Thai Me Up in Edinburgh

4 Picardy Place ☎0131/558 9234, ⊛www.tmeup.com. Closed for lunch Sun–Tues. Not the most convincing of names, but the Thai cooking is fresh, dynamic and colourful. The moderately priced menu is short and to the point, with specialities including steamed fish and beef in red curry sauce, and the "authentic" Thai artefacts are subtle enough to allow the food to take centre stage.

Pubs and bars

The Barony Bar

81–85 Broughton St ☎0131/557 0546. Mon–Fri & Sun 11am–midnight, Sat 11am–1am. A fine old-fashioned bar which manages to be big and lively without being spoilt. Chainification has blunted a bit of its appeal, but there's still real ale and a blazing fire.

The Basement

10a–12a Broughton St. ☎0131/557 0097, ⊛www.thebasement.org. uk. Daily noon–1am. This dimly lit, grungy drinking hole has long been a favourite of the Bohemian Broughton Street crowd, with odd furniture made from old JCBs and filling food served by Hawaiian-shirted staff.

The Outhouse

14 Broughton St Lane ☎0131/557 6668. Daily 11am–1am. Busy pre-club bar tucked away down a cobbled lane off Broughton Street, with a lively beer garden and funky music.

Pivo

2–6 Calton Rd ☎0131/557 2925. Daily 4pm–3am. Decent small-hours drinking den with DJs every night and a pretty mellow clientele – the Czech theme begins and just about ends with the name.

Planet Out

6 Baxter's Place (Leith Walk) ☎0131/524 0061. Daily 4pm–1am. The liveliest of the local gay bars, this revs up fairly late, with DJs doing a pre-club routine.

PLACES Calton Hill and Broughton

Along the Water of Leith

Edinburgh's fairly placid Water of Leith is little more than a stream, but as it meanders through the city's northern suburbs, its course links various important sights, including the city's most dynamic art galleries, the tranquil Botanic Garden and the suburban villages of Dean and Stockbridge. Within walking distance of the city centre, and with a pleasant walkway running along the banks of the river, this stretch of the city makes a delightfully verdant escape from uptown's bustle and traffic, with both indoor and outdoor attractions, a good mixture of culture and nature, and plenty of attractive cafés, bars and restaurants.

Water of Leith Walkway

@www.waterofleith.org.uk. Stretching thirteen miles along the entire length of the Water of Leith, this well-signposted walkway is easy to pick up along short sections where it runs through Edinburgh's northern suburbs, transporting you very quickly from the grand architecture of the New Town to a wooded gorge filled with the sounds of gurgling water and birdsong.

The stretch heading west from Stockbridge past the Dean Village to the Dean Gallery is both a practical route between these spots, and a prettily varied walk through the deepest part of the gorge which passes a series of attractive old buildings, including St Bernard's Well, a Classical folly built over a mineral spring. In previous centuries the river was heavily polluted by the New Town's sewage and up to 100 different mills and small factories which were established along its length; today you might see a fisherman trying his luck on one of the slower stretches of the stream.

Royal Botanic Garden

Inverleith Row ☎0131/552 7171, @www.rbge.org.uk. Daily: Nov–Feb 10am–4pm, till 6pm March/Oct, till 7pm April–Sept. Free, £3.50 entry to glasshouses. Guided tours (April–Sept 11am & 2pm; 1.5hrs; £3) start at the West Gate on Arboretum Place. Established on this seventy-acre site on the northern side of the Water of Leith in 1820, and filled with mature trees and

▲ BOTANIC GARDEN EAST GATES

a huge variety of native and exotic plants and flowers, the "botanics" (as they're commonly called) are most popular simply as a place to stroll and lounge around on the grass. Towards the eastern side of the gardens, a series of ten glasshouses include the elegant 1850s Palm House, and a contrasting 1960s design with a complex exterior frame of struts and tensioners intended to maximise the amount of light and avoid the need for internal pillars. Inside, there's a steamy array of palms, ferns, orchids, cycads and aquatic plants, including some huge circular water lilies. Elsewhere in the garden, different themes are highlighted: the large Chinese-style garden, for example, has a bubbling waterfall and the world's biggest collection of Chinese wild plants outside China, while in the northwest corner there's a Scottish native woodland which very effectively evokes the wild unkemptness of parts of the Scottish Highlands and west coast. Art is also a strong theme within the botanics, with a gallery showing changing contemporary exhibitions within the attractive eighteenth-century Inverleith House

at the centre of the gardens and, scattered all around, a number of outdoor sculptures, including a giant pine cone by landscape artist Andy Goldsworthy and the striking stainless-steel east gate, designed in the form of stylized rhododendrons. Parts of the garden are also notable for some great vistas: the busy *Terrace Café* (see p.131) beside Inverleith House offers one of the city's best views of the castle and Old Town's steeples and monuments.

Stockbridge

First established around the Water of Leith ford (and seventeenth century bridge) over which cattle were driven to market in Edinburgh, Stockbridge was essentially gobbled up in the expansion of the New Town, but a few charming buildings and an independent character prevail in the district today. It's a popular quarter for young professionals who can't afford the soaring property prices in the New Town proper, and as a result there's a good crop of bars, boutiques and places to eat along both Raeburn Place, the main road, and St Stephen Street, long one of Edinburgh's more offbeat side-streets and a great place for some shopping or a drink or bite to eat.

▼ ARCHWAY TO FROMER STOCKBRIDGE MARKET

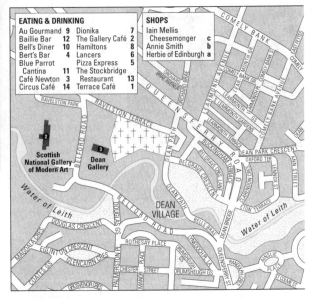

EATING & DRINKING			
Au Gourmand	9	Dionika	7
Baillie Bar	12	The Gallery Café	2
Bell's Diner	10	Hamiltons	8
Bert's Bar	4	Lancers	6
Blue Parrot		Pizza Express	5
Cantina	11	The Stockbridge	
Café Newton	3	Restaurant	13
Circus Café	14	Terrace Café	1

SHOPS	
Iain Mellis	
Cheesemonger	c
Annie Smith	b
Herbie of Edinburgh	a

Dean Village

Less than half a mile upstream from Stockbridge the gorge of the Water of Leith becomes noticeably deep and steep. Nestled into the banks here, the old milling community of Dean Village is one of central Edinburgh's most picturesque – yet oddest – corners, its atmosphere of decay arrested by the conversion of numerous granaries and tall mill buildings into designer flats. More recent

▼DEAN VILLAGE HOUSE

buildings have mimicked the style of the mills to maintain a sense of heritage and individuality, and the area makes a picturesque detour from the Water of Leith walkway. Surviving features of the Victorian community include the school, clocktower and communal drying green, while high above the Dean Village is Dean Bridge, a bravura feat of 1830s engineering by Thomas Telford, which carries the main road over 100 feet above the river.

Scottish National Gallery of Modern Art

75 Belford Rd ☎ 0131/624 6200, ⓦ www.natgalscot.ac.uk. Daily 10am–5pm, plus late-opening Thurs till 7pm. Free. Accessed from the Water of Leith Walkway via a long, steep set of steps, the Scottish National Gallery of Modern Art was the first collection in Britain devoted solely to twentieth-

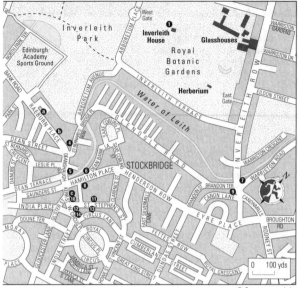

© Crown copyright

century painting and sculpture. It operates in tandem with Dean Gallery across the road (see p.130); both galleries are located in impressive Neoclassical buildings which have been superbly converted into pleasant, relaxing viewing spaces, and both also have excellent cafés – if it's a sunny day head for the one at the Gallery of Modern Art, which has a verdant outdoor terrace. The extensive wooded grounds of both galleries serve as a sculpture park, featuring works by Jacob Epstein, Henry Moore, Barbara Hepworth and, most strikingly, Charles Jencks, whose prize-winning *Landform*, a swirling mix of ponds and grassy mounds, dominates the area in front of the Gallery of Modern Art. In contrast, there are few permanent works inside – one exception is Douglas Gordon's *List of Names (Random)*, an examination of "how our heads function", which lists in plain

▼GALLERY CAFÉ, SCOTTISH NATIONAL GALLERY OF MODERN ART

type on a white wall everyone the artist can remember meeting. Otherwise, the display space is divided between temporary exhibitions and selections from the gallery's own holdings; the latter are arranged thematically, but are almost constantly moved

Getting to the galleries

If you're heading directly to the Modern Art and Dean galleries from the city centre, you can jump on the free special bus service, which runs on the hour (Mon–Sat 11am–5pm, Sun noon–5pm) from outside the National Gallery on the Mound, stopping at the National Portrait Gallery on the way. The only regular public transport running along Belford Road is bus #13, which leaves from the western end of George Street.

around. The collections starts with early twentieth century Post-Impressionists, then moves through the Fauves, German Expressionism, Cubism and Pop Art, with works by Lichtenstein and Warhol establishing a connection with the extensive holdings of Paolozzi's work in the Dean Gallery. There's a strong section on British artists, from Francis Bacon and Gilbert & George to Britart exponents such as Damien Hirst and Rachel Whiteread, while modern Scottish art ranges from the Colourists – whose works are attracting ever-growing posthumous critical acclaim – to the distinctive styles of contemporary Scots such as John Bellany, a portraitist of striking originality, and the poet–artist–gardener Ian Hamilton Finlay.

Dean Gallery

72 Belford Rd ☎ 0131/624 6200, ⊛ www.natgalscot.ac.uk. Daily Mon–Sun 10am–5pm, plus late-opening Thurs till 7pm. Free. The latest addition to the National Galleries of Scotland, the Dean is housed in a former orphanage which was dramatically refurbished specifically to make room for the work of Edinburgh-born sculptor Sir Eduardo Paolozzi, described by some as the father of Pop Art. The collection was partly assembled from a bequest by Gabrielle Keiller, and partly from a gift of the artist himself which included some 3000 sculptures, 2000 prints and drawings and 3000 books.

There's an awesome introduction to Paolozzi's work by the huge *Vulcan*, a half-man, half-machine which squeezes into the Great Hall immediately opposite the main entrance – view it both from ground level and from the head-height balcony to appreciate the sheer scale of the piece. No less persuasive of Paolozzi's dynamic creative talents are the rooms to the right of the main entrance, where his London studio has been expertly recreated right down to the clutter of half-finished casts, toys and empty pots of glue. Hidden amongst this chaos is a large part of his bequest, with incomplete models piled four or five deep on the floor and designs stacked randomly on shelves. The ground floor also holds the Roland Penrose Gallery's world-renowned collection of Dada and Surrealist art; Penrose was a close friend and patron of many of the movements' leading figures, and Marcel Duchamp, Max Ernst and Man Ray are all represented. Look out also for Dalí's *The Signal of Anguish* and Magritte's *Magic Mirror* along with work by Miró and Giacometti – all hung on crowded walls with an assortment of artefacts and ethnic souvenirs gathered by Penrose and his artist companions while travelling.

The rooms upstairs are normally given over to special and touring exhibitions, which usually carry an entrance charge.

Shops

Iain Mellis Cheesemonger

6 Bakers Place ☎0131/225 6566, ⓦwww.ijmellischeesemonger.com. Superb cave of farmhouse cheeses – the quality and range are impeccable, and in foodie Stockbridge it's not unusual to see a queue out the door.

Annie Smith

20 Raeburn Place ☎0131/332 5749. Closed Sun. One of a number of art and craft galleries in Stockbridge, with rings, bracelets and other attractive jewellery handmade on the premises.

Herbie of Edinburgh

66 Raeburn Place. Closed Sun. Tiny if much-loved deli which has held its own by sourcing top-quality cheese, olives and wine. Best known for the wheel of ripe, gooey brie de meaux that sits on top of the display counter.

Cafés

Au Gourmand

1 Brandon Terrace ☎0131/624 4666. French-owned and unmistakably French-flavoured café with a handful of deli items on sale, a bakery downstairs and some tables at the back. Great for patisserie, sandwiches and crepes.

Café Newton

Dean Gallery, 72 Belford Rd. Daily 10am–4.30pm. The better of the two cafés within the Dean and Modern Art galleries, with a high corniced ceiling and table service adding a touch of refinement. Filled focaccia as well as with daily specials and excellent cakes are on offer.

Circus Café

15 North West Circus Place ☎0131/220 0333. An ultra-chic bank conversion with impeccable foodie credentials: a deli and wine shop in the basement, and an upstairs café that's open until 11pm and makes use of the best of the produce with platters, salads and moderately priced main dishes.

The Gallery Café

Scottish National Gallery of Modern Art, 74 Belford Rd ☎0131/332 8600. Far more than a standard refreshment stop for gallery visitors, the cultured setting (which includes a lovely outside eating area) and appealing menu of hearty soups, healthy salads and filled croissants pulls in reassuring numbers of locals.

Terrace Café

Royal Botanic Garden ☎0131/552 0616. A great location right in the middle of the garden, with outside tables offering stunning views of the city skyline, but the food isn't that exciting and it can be busy (and noisy) with families.

Restaurants

Bell's Diner

7 St Stephen's St ☎0131/225 8116. An unpretentious front-room

restaurant with a simple mid-priced menu of home-made burgers, decent steaks and pancakes. It's only open in the evenings (plus Saturday lunch) and is a longstanding local favourite, so tables aren't easy to come by.

Blue Parrot Cantina

49 St Stephen's St ☏0131/225 2941. Evenings only. Cosy, quirky, moderately priced basement Mexican restaurant, with a frequently changing evening menu that makes a decent effort to deviate from the predictable clichés via house specialities such as *pescado baja* (haddock with a creamy lime sauce).

Dionika

3–6 Canonmills Bridge ☏0131/652 3993. Daily 9am–10.30pm. Deli, restaurant and tapas bar near the Botanic Gardens, with a strong Spanish accent; the star turn is the seafood paella prepared every lunchtime and evening in a corner of the dining area.

Lancers

5 Hamilton Place ☏0131/332 3444. A reliable old-school Indian restaurant serving mostly rich, filling Bengali and Punjabi curries at moderate prices.

Pizza Express

1 Deanhaugh St ☏0131/332 7229, ☏www.pizzaexpress.co.uk. The chain with the winning formula for smart interiors and decent pizzas comes up trumps with a terrific location in a clocktower building nuzzled right beside the Water of Leith.

The Stockbridge Restaurant

54 St Stephen's St ☏0131/226 6766. Closed Sun. Rather upmarket and expensive, this enveloping dining space is open only in the evenings and serves up modern Scottish dishes, with much of the produce sourced from the nearby butchers, fishmongers and delis.

Pubs and bars

Bailie Bar

2 St Stephen's St ☏0131/225 4673. Sun–Thurs 11am–midnight, Fri & Sat 11am–1am. The best of the district's traditional pubs, with English and Scottish ales as well as better-than-average pub grub.

Bert's Bar

2–4 Raeburn Place ☏0131/332 6345. Sun–Thurs 11am–midnight, Fri & Sat 11am–1am. Popular locals' pub with a lived-in feel, despite their relatively recent arrival. Serves excellent beer, tasty pies and strives to be an authentic, non-theme-oriented venue, though the telly rarely misses any sporting action.

Hamiltons Bar & Kitchen

16–18 Hamilton Place ☏0131/226 4199, ☏www.hamiltonsbar.com. Mon-Sat11am–1am, Sun 11am–midnight. One of the few self-proclaimed gastropubs in the city, where the food is of equal importance to the booze. Expect blonde wood fittings and sea bass with your chips.

▼BAILIE BAR LAMP

Leith

Although Leith is generally known as the port of Edinburgh, it developed independently of the city up the hill, its history bound up in the hard graft of fishing, shipbuilding and trade. The presence of sailors, merchants and continental traders gave the place a cosmopolitan – if slightly rough – edge, which is still obvious today in Leith's fascinating mix of cobbled streets and flash new housing, container ships and historic buildings, ugly council flats and trendy waterside bistros. While the stand-alone attractions are few, Leith is an intriguing place to explore, worth visiting not just for the contrasts to central Edinburgh, but also for its nautical air and the excellent eating and drinking scene, which majors on seafood but also includes haute cuisine and well-worn, friendly pubs.

▲PUB SIGN, THE SHORE

Leith Links

An area of predominantly flat parkland on the eastern side of Leith, the clue to Leith Links' place in history is (to golfers at least) in the name. Documentary evidence from 1505 suggests that James IV used to "play at gowf at Leithe", giving rise to Leith's claim as the birthplace of the sport. In 1744 the first written rules of golf were drawn up here by the Honourable Company of Edinburgh Golfers, ten years before they were formalized in St Andrews. Golf fans keen to pay homage to the spot may be a little disappointed, however: the only recognition given to this piece of sporting history is a commemorative cairn beside Duncan Place showing the layout of the original five-hole course, and other than informal practice sessions by locals, there's no golf played on the Links these days. Instead, the tree-lined area of municipal park offers a stretch of green space for a walk or a play around.

Trinity House

99 Kirkgate ☎0131/554 3289, ◉www.historic-scotland.gov.uk. £2. While Leith has a fair number of interesting old buildings, many are tucked away or obscured by more recent developments, and few are given the prominence accorded to architectural and historical treasures elsewhere in the city. Trinity House is the

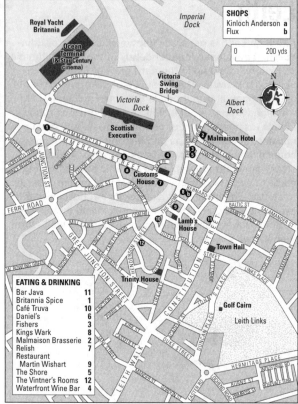

SHOPS
Kinloch Anderson   a
Flux   b

0   200 yds

EATING & DRINKING

Bar Java	11
Britannia Spice	1
Café Truva	10
Daniel's	6
Fishers	3
Kings Wark	8
Malmaison Brasserie	2
Relish	7
Restaurant Martin Wishart	9
The Shore	5
The Vintner's Rooms	12
Waterfront Wine Bar	4

© Crown copyright

only one of the port's grand buildings open to the public, but even here access is limited – all visits must be pre-booked on the number above, but if you're interested in maritime history, it's well worth the effort. The house is home of the Incorporation of Masters and Mariners of Leith, and was used in the medieval era as a mariners' hospice, funded by a tax on ships coming into the port. The present Neoclassical villa dates from 1816 and has some impressive original interiors and plasterwork, as well a significant collection of maritime memorabilia, paintings and ships' models.

The Shore

The best way to absorb Leith's history and seafaring connections is to take a stroll along the Shore, a tenement-lined road running alongside the final stretch of the Water of Leith, just before it disgorges into the working docks area and, beyond that, the Firth of Forth. Until the mid-nineteenth century this was a bustling and cosmopolitan harbour, visited by ships from all over the world, but as vessels docking here became increasingly large, they moored up instead at custom-built docks built beyond the original quays; these days, the Shore has only a handful of boats permanently moored alongside. Instead, the focus of the Shore is on the numerous pubs and restaurants which line the street, many of which spill tables and chairs out onto the cobbled pavement on sunny days. A drink or snack at one of these places (see pp.136–8) is a great way to absorb the scene, but if you're taking a gentle amble along the length of the Shore it's well worth checking out some of the historic buildings, too, which include the imposing Neoclassical Custom House, still used as offices by the harbour authority (though not open to the public); the round signal tower above *Fishers* restaurant, which was originally constructed as a windmill; and the turrets and towers of the Sailors' Home, built in Scots Baronial style in the 1880s as a dosshouse for seafarers, and now home to the rather swankier digs of the *Malmaison Hotel* (see p.166). If you walk on from here past the heavy steel girders of the 130-year-old Victoria Swing Bridge you'll get a good view of today's working docks, a mix of old warehouses, container loading bays and the seeming unstoppable march of new housing.

Royal Yacht Britannia

Ocean Drive ☎0131/555 5566, ⊛www.royalyachtbritannia.co.uk. Daily: March–Oct 9.30am–4.30pm; Nov–Feb 10am–3.30pm. £9. Moored alongside Terence Conran's huge Ocean Terminal shopping and entertainment centre, *Britannia* is one of the world's most famous ships. Launched in 1953, she was used by the royal family over 44 years for state visits, diplomatic functions, honeymoons and holidays; Leith's port operators acquired her following decommission in 1997 against the wishes of many of the royals, who felt that scuttling would have been a more dignified end. Visits to *Britannia* begin in the visitor centre within Ocean Terminal, where royal holiday snaps and video clips of *Britannia* in various exotic foreign ports are shown. After this you're allowed on board, with the chance to wander around the bridge, admiral's quarters, officers' mess and state apartments. The ship has been largely kept as she was when in service, with a well-preserved 1950s dowdiness which the audioguide loyally attributes to the Queen's good taste and astute frugality in the lean postwar years. Certainly the atmosphere is a far cry from the opulent splendour which many expect.

While *Britannia* will inevitably captivate ardent royalists, the tour offers some entertaining insights into life aboard even if you're not into loyal veneration: a full Marine Band was always

▼ROYAL YACHT BRITANNIA

part of the 300-strong crew; hand signals were used by the sailors to communicate orders as shouting was forbidden; and a special solid mahogany rail was built onto the royal bridge to allow the Queen to stand on deck as *Britannia* came into port, without fear of a gust of wind lifting the royal skirt.

Newhaven

To the west of Leith lies the old village (now suburb) of Newhaven, established by James IV at the start of the sixteenth century as an alternative shipbuilding centre to Leith: his massive warship, the *Great Michael*, capable of carrying 120 gunners, 300 mariners and 1000 troops, and said to have used up all the trees in Fife, was built here. Newhaven has also been a ferry station and an important fishing centre, landing some six million oysters a year at the height of its success in the 1860s. Today, the chief pleasure here is a stroll around the stone harbour, which still has a pleasantly salty feel with a handful of boats tied up alongside or resting gently on the tidal mud. You might want to make a brief stop at the small Newhaven Heritage Museum (daily noon–4.45pm; free), which has a fairly home-spun series of exhibits about the district's history of fishing and seafaring.

Shops

Kinloch Anderson

Commercial St ☎0131/555 1390, ⊛www.kinlochanderson.com. Closed Sun. One of Edinburgh's larger kilt outfitters, with a large showroom full of tartan and the associated trimmings. Fairly conservative, so don't go in hoping to get hold of the *Braveheart* look.

Flux

55 Bernard St ☎0131/554 4075. Closed Mon. Interesting local arts and crafts, including pottery and funky glass lampshades as well as more mainstream, gimmicky knick-knacks.

Ocean Terminal

Ocean Drive ☎0131/558 8888, ⊛www .oceanterminal.com. Leith's big retail destination, though with Debenhams and BHS as the headline department stores, it's not the most exciting shopping spot in the city. However, the presence of Gap, Kurt Muller, Fat Face and the FairTrade store Earth Squared makes things a bit more interesting.

Cafés

Café Truva

77 The Shore ☎0131/554 5502. Surprisingly, café culture hasn't

▼SHIP IN DOCK, LEITH HARBOUR

really made it to Leith, but this
Turkish-owned place just back
from the water serves up decent
sandwiches and snacks, as well as
coffee made both in the Italian
and in the Turkish way.

Relish

6 Commercial St ☎ 0131/476 1920.
Leith's best deli, with some
excellent cheeses, hams and
treats if you want to make up
your own sandwiches. The
window stools are a nice spot
for a coffee or a treat.

Restaurants

Britannia Spice

150 Commercial St ☎ 0131/555
2255, ⊛ www.britanniaspice.co.uk.
Closed Sun lunch. The decor has
a nautical theme; the decent,
mid-priced food is prepared by
specialist chefs from different
parts of the subcontinent; and
the awards for this relatively
new but ambitious Indian
restaurant have been piling up.

Daniel's

88 Commercial St ☎ 0131/553 5933,
⊛ www.daniels-bistro.co.uk. Likeable,
well-run bistro in an attractive
setting on the ground floor of
a converted warehouse. Food
is heartily French, with many
dishes from the Alsace; the
tarte flambée, one of the house
specialities, is a simple but
delicious onion and bacon pizza.

Fishers

1 The Shore ☎ 0131/554 5666,
⊛ www.fishersbistros.co.uk. One
of the first wave of seafood
bistros which put Leith's dining
scene on the map, the menu
here has an appealing range of
expensive and fancy fish dishes,
but there are also impressive
bar-style snacks such as fishcakes

▲ VINTNERS ROOMS

and chowder. Reservations
recommended.

Malmaison Brasserie

1 Tower Place ☎ 0131/468 5001,
⊛ www.malmaison.com. A successful
attempt to re-create the feel
of a stylish Parisian restaurant,
serving excellent steak and chips
as well as indulgent breakfasts
and brunches.

Restaurant Martin Wishart

54 The Shore ☎ 0131/553 3557,
⊛ www.martin-wishart.co.uk. Closed
Sat lunch, Sun & Mon. One of
only two Michelin-starred
restaurants in Edinburgh, this
place wows the gourmets
with highly accomplished,
French-influenced Scottish
food (three-course lunch for
under £20, six-course evening
tasting menu at £55). The food
is incredible, though the decor is
rather beige. Reservations
recommended.

The Shore

3–4 The Shore ☎ 0131/553 5080. A
long-established bar/restaurant
with huge mirrors, wood

panelling and aproned waiters who serve up fine fish dishes and decent wines.

The Vintner's Rooms

87 Giles St ☎0131/5546767, ✆www .thevintnersrooms.com. Closed Sun evening & Mon. Splendid restaurant in a seventeenth-century warehouse; the small but ornate Rococo dining room is a marvel, and the food isn't bad either; expect to pay £15–20 for mains such as wild halibut in saffron broth or peppered venison.

Waterfront Wine Bar

1c Dock Place ☎0131/554 7427. Tasty seafood dishes, mostly mid-priced and not too fussy, served in a former lock-keeper's cottage which has been extended over the water to create a New England-style effect. You can eat in the wonderfully characterful wine bar (smoking) or non-smoking conservatory at the back.

Pubs and bars

Bar Java

48–52 Constitution St ☎0131/553 2020, ✆www.hotelbarjava.com. Daily 11am–1am. Friendly, modern bar in an area where you'd expect all the pubs to have sawdust on the floor. Decent food and a small courtyard beer garden.

Kings Wark

36 The Shore ☎0131/554 9260. Sun–Thurs noon–11pm, Fri & Sat noon–midnight. Real ale in an atmospheric, restored eighteenth-century pub in prime position on the Shore, with impressive bar meals chalked up on the rafters.

The Shore

3–4 The Shore ☎0131/553 5080. Mon–Sat 11am–midnight, Sun 12.30–11pm. Atmospheric traditional bar with an adjacent restaurant (see p.137). There's regular live jazz or folk music as well as real ales and good bar snacks.

▲WATERFRONT WINE BAR

North and west Edinburgh

The sights and attractions to the north and west of Edinburgh's compact centre are more widely spread out, but the open spaces here provide a welcome break from the sometimes overwhelming history and architecture of the centre, and there's also the chance to discover the capital's seafront. The principal landmark on this side of the city is wooded Corstorphine Hill, whose lower slopes harbour Edinburgh Zoo, one of the city's most popular family attractions. Nearby there's Murrayfield Stadium, the largest sporting arena in the city, and Edinburgh's last working brewery. Another of the villages now absorbed into Edinburgh, Cramond lies at the mouth of the River Almond and makes a great base for a bracing shoreline walk.

Edinburgh Zoo

Corstorphine Rd, Corstorphine ☎0131/334 9171, ⊛www.edinburghzoo .org.uk. Daily: April–Sept 9am–6pm; Oct & March 9am–5pm; Nov–Feb 9am–4.30pm. £8.50. Buses #12, #26 & #31 from Princes St, or #100 from Waverley Bridge. Established in 1913, Edinburgh's zoo has a long-established reputation for preserving rare and endangered species. The eighty-acre site is permanently packed with kids, and many of the facilities are imaginatively designed with education as well as play in mind – the climbing frame's position near the chimps enclosure allows parents to keep half an eye on both, and reflect on Edinburgh student Charles Darwin's theories of evolution. The general emphasis of the zoo is fast moving away from bored animals in cages to imaginatively designed habitats and viewing areas — the latter are best seen by taking a hilltop safari, a regular shuttle trip to the top of Corstorphine

▲PENGUIN PARADE, EDINBURGH ZOO

Hill in a Landrover-pulled trailer, which passes large enclosures

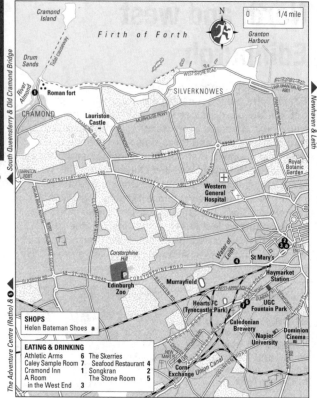

SHOPS
Helen Bateman Shoes **a**

EATING & DRINKING
Athletic Arms	6	The Skerries	
Caley Sample Room	7	Seafood Restaurant	4
Cramond Inn	1	Songkran	2
A Room		The Stone Room	5
in the West End	3		

© Crown copyright

full of camels and llamas. Once at the top, you can admire the city views, then wander back down past the African Plains Experience – an elevated wooden walkway out past some zebra and antelope grazing in fields which are, admittedly, rather more Midlothian than Maasai Mara – and a row of glass-walled pens containing various species of big cat. The zoo's most famous inhabitants are its penguins, a legacy of Leith's whaling trade in the South Atlantic. The penguin parade, which takes place daily at 2.15pm from April to September, and on sunny March and October days, has gained

something of a cult status, with rangers encouraging a bunch of the flightless birds to leave their pen and waddle around a short circuit of pathways thronged with admiring and amused spectators.

Caledonian Brewery

48 Slateford Rd, Gorgie ☎0131/337 1286, ⊛www.caledonian-brewery .co.uk. Buses #34 & #44 from Princes St. Occupying a network of red-brick buildings and long, low storehouses wedged in beside a railway line, the Caledonian is the last brewery of significant size still operating in Edinburgh. It was established in 1869, when there were around forty

breweries in the city, and despite the march of technology and shift in drinking preferences, it's still concocting its signature 80 shilling and Deuchar's IPA ales using largely traditional methods. Tours of this very small-scale operation (arrange in advance on the number above) offer a chance to see the key elements of the brewing process close up, including the hop room, fermentation and the last direct-fired brewing coppers still in use in the UK – a particular highlight for brewing aficionados, as they're said to impart a distinctive flavour to Caledonian's beers. There's a lively beer festival held at the brewery in June each year, and one of the warehouses has been converted into a hall where ceilidhs are held on Saturday nights (☎0131/228 5688; 8pm–1am; £6).

Murrayfield Stadium

Roseburn St, Murrayfield ☎0131/346 5000, ⊛www.scottishrugby.org. Buses #12, #26, #31 from Princes St. Well-known to rugby union fans around the world, Murrayfield is where Scotland's home international fixtures are played. An impressive all-seat stadium holding 68,000 people, it's an exciting place to be when packed to the gills with singing, chanting fans on match-days, and has an equally inspiring feel when empty; guided tours (book 48hrs in advance; £5) offer a chance to poke around a few of the forbidden quarters of the arena, with a look at the commentary boxes, hospitality areas, dressing rooms and tunnel, concluding with a chance to take a player's-eye-view by walking (or running) out through the tunnel. A shop in the stadium concourse (Mon–Sat 9am–5pm) sells replica shirts, sports gear and souvenirs.

Lauriston Castle

Cramond Rd South, Davidson's Mains ☎0131/336 2060, ⊛www.cac.org .uk. Admission by tour only: April–Oct Sat–Thurs 11.20am, 12.20pm, 2.20pm, 3.20pm, 4.20pm; Nov–March Sat & Sun 12.20pm, 3.20pm. £4.50. Bus #24 from Princes or Frederick streets. A country villa set in its own parkland on the fringes of Edinburgh's northwest urban sprawl, Lauriston Castle is a well-preserved, if fairly unglamorous, oddity. On first sight a neo-Jacobean riot of pointy turrets, crow-stepped gables and tall, thin chimneys, the "castle" is in fact a late sixteenth-century tower-house with extensive domestic additions from the 1820s and 1870s. At the turn of the twentieth century it was bought by a well-to-do Edinburgh couple, Mr and Mrs Reid, who upgraded and furnished it with all the mod cons of the early Edwardian era, including hot and cold running water, central heating and double glazing. They also

▼CALEDONIAN BREWERY

▲LAURISTON CASTLE

filled the building with objects they liked or found technically accomplished, including some fine Italian furniture, Blue John glassware and seventeenth-century Dutch tapestries. On the death of Mrs Reid, the house and contents were gifted to Edinburgh Council, and have been preserved as a time capsule of that era. The mature grounds include an ornamental Japanese friendship garden and a series of croquet lawns from where there are pleasantly sylvan views out over Firth of Forth.

Cramond

Buses #24 and #41 from George St. Clustered on the eastern bank of the River Almond where it meets the Forth estuary, Cramond is one of the city's most atmospheric – and poshest – old villages. Popular with locals for Sunday afternoon seaside strolls, it's a great place to take in some sea air and explore the compact but charming series of step-gabled whitewashed houses which rise up from the riverside, interlaced with steep alleys and stairways. The best of the local walks are along the wide promenade which

follows the shoreline, from where you get some great views of the Forth; or out across the causeway to the uninhabited bird sanctuary of Cramond Island – though be aware that the causeway disappears as high tide approaches and can leave you stranded if you get your timings wrong. For tide times, either check the noticeboard on shore (although this is sometimes vandalized) or call the Coastguard (☎01333/450 666). Inland of Cramond, there's another pleasant walk along a tree-lined path leading upstream along the River Almond, past

▼CRAMOND PROMENADE

former mills and their adjoining cottages towards the sixteenth-century Old Cramond Bridge.

Ratho Adventure Centre

South Platt Hill, Ratho ☎0131/333 6333, ⊛www.adventurescotland.com. Mon–Fri 10.30am–10.30pm, Sat & Sun 9.30am–8pm. Free entry; charges for activities vary. Undoubtedly one of the modern wonders of Scotland, the Adventure Centre was opened in 2003 at a cost of over £24 million and is the world's largest indoor climbing arena, incorporating a remarkable 2400 square metres of artificial climbing wall. The spectacular vision of its architect founders was to enclose (and roof) a disused quarry, creating a giant arena that's now used for international climbing competitions as well as classes (from £20 for an hour-long taster session) for climbers of all levels, including beginners and kids. Above the arena, just under the glass roof, is the SkyRide (£8), a stomach-churning aerial obstacle course 100 feet off the ground, which you take on secured into a sliding harness. Elsewhere in this multi-faceted facility are a state-of-the-art gym, scuba diving facilities, mountain bike routes, accommodation and a decent restaurant and café which peers out over the climbing arena. Most of the facilities, including the climbing walls, artificial boulders and SkyRide, can be used on a "Pay-2-Play" basis (£8, plus £3 daily registration), with taster sessions and teaching available.

At the time of going to press no public transport linked to the centre; if you're driving, follow the signs from the Newbridge roundabout on the A8, not far from the airport.

Shops

Helen Bateman Shoes

16 William St, West End ☎0131/220 4495, ⊛www.helenbateman.com. Closed Sun. A chic boutique selling an exquisite range of designer and bespoke ladies shoes. As sexy in the city as it gets in Edinburgh.

Restaurants

The Skerries Seafood Restaurant

Dunstane House Hotel, 4 West Coates, Haymarket ☎0131/337 5320, ⊛www.dunstanehousehotel.co.uk. Closed Mon–Fri lunch. Meat and (memorably) seafood direct from the verdant shores of the Orkney Isles, available both in the bar and in the smarter, more expensive hotel restaurant.

The Stone Room

The Adventure Centre, Ratho ☎0131/333 6333, ⊛www .adventurescotland.com. Decent restaurant, bar and café that feels

▼RATHO ADVENTURE CENTRE

a bit like an upmarket ski lodge and serves up all the sorts of things you'd want after scaling the equivalent of the north face of the Eiger: healthy salads, wholesome pizzas or clean-tasting fish and meat dishes.

A Room in the West End

26 William St, West End ☎0131/226 1036, ⓦwww.aroomin.co.uk/westend. Closed Sun lunch. Basement dining area where you'll find a convivial atmosphere and reasonably priced, Scottish-themed food such as haggis, neeps and tatties, or loin of pork with black pudding.

Songkran

24a Stafford St, West End ☎0131/225 7889, ⓦwww.songkran.co.uk. Closed Sun lunch. A fairly straightforward but reliable Thai restaurant squeezed into a basement dining room. The long menu of Thai staples is moderately priced, with banquet options under £20 per head and lunch under £10.

Pubs and bars

Athletic Arms (The Diggers)

1–3 Angle Park Terrace, Gorgie ☎0131/337 3822. Mon–Thurs noon–midnight, Fri & Sat noon–1am, Sun 12.30–6pm. Known to all as *The Diggers* after the spade-wielding employees of the cemetery across the road, this is a place of pilgrimage if you're into sport (Murrayfield and Heart's Tyncastle ground are just along the road) and real ale, with the Caledonian Brewery's beers well represented.

Caley Sample Room

58 Angle Park Terrace, Gorgie ☎0131/337 7204. Sun–Thurs 11am–midnight, Fri & Sat 11am–1am. Showcase pub for the cask ales of the nearby Caledonian Brewery, though it gets fearsomely thronged when there's a big game at Murrayfield.

Cramond Inn

30 Cramond Glebe Rd, Cramond ☎0131/336 2035. Mon–Thurs 11am–11pm; Fri & Sat 11am–midnight, Sun 12.30–11pm. This old inn by the riverside at Cramond is the perfect place for a drink or a pub meal after a stroll along the coastal path.

South Edinburgh

South Edinburgh begins at the open spaces of the Meadows, just beyond the University, from where suburbs stretch out to old Midlothian mining towns and the significant elevation of the Pentland Hills. The leafy, mainly Victorian suburbs closest to town hold many student digs and guesthouses, although there's no doubt that the refined essence of Miss Jean Brodie, who was in her prime in this part of town, lingers on. Beyond these, the green patches of the south's numerous hills offer some pleasant walking routes, though you'll need to catch a bus to get out to the most interesting of the sights, the Rosslyn Chapel, Scotland's most mysterious medieval church.

The Meadows

Like the Old Town's Princes Street Gardens (see p.105), the area of parkland known as the Meadows was once a shallow loch. Drained in the eighteenth century, its sheltered swathes of grass are well utilized for games of tennis, cricket and football, though they're just as popular as a pleasant through-route to or from the Southside, with lovely blossoms appearing on the trees in spring and grand views up to Arthur's Seat. On the southwest corner of the Meadows is the slightly more elevated land of Bruntsfield Links, another of Edinburgh's early golf courses, which now operates as a 36-hole pitch-and-putt course in the summer (April–Sept; free; clubs and balls can be hired from the Golf Tavern; see p.150).

Craigmillar Castle

Craigmillar Castle Rd, Craigmillar ☏0131/661 4445, ⊛www.historic -scotland.co.uk. April–Sept daily 9.30am–6pm; Oct–March Sat–Wed 9.30am–4pm. £2.50. Bus #30, #33 or #82 from North Bridge to Little France, then a ten-minute walk along Craigmillar Castle Rd. Set in

a green belt around five miles southeast of Edinburgh's centre, Craigmillar is one of the best-preserved medieval fortresses in Scotland. Before Queen Victoria set her heart on Balmoral, it was considered her royal castle

▼STROLLERS IN THE MEADOWS

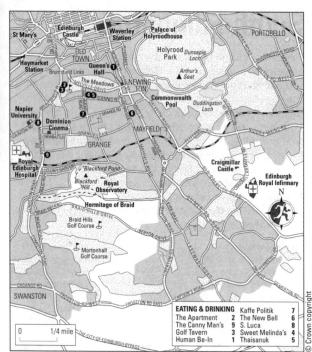

EATING & DRINKING		Kaffe Politik	7
The Apartment	2	The New Bell	6
The Canny Man's	9	S. Luca	8
Golf Tavern	3	Sweet Melinda's	4
Human Be-In	1	Thaisanuk	5

© Crown copyright

Pentland Hills, Hillend ▼ *& Flotterstone*   *Rosslyn Chapel* ▼ *& Penicuik*   *Mining Museum* ▼ *& Dalkeith*

north of the border, a possibility which seems somewhat odd now given its proximity to the ugly council housing scheme of Craigmillar, one of Edinburgh's most deprived districts. That said, the immediate setting feels very rural and Craigmillar enjoys splendid views back to Arthur's Seat and Edinburgh Castle. The oldest part of the complex is the L-shaped tower house, which dates back to the early 1400s – this remains substantially intact, and the great hall, with its resplendent late Gothic chimneypiece, is in good enough shape to be rented out for functions. The tower house was surrounded in the 1500s by a quadrangular wall with cylindrical corner towers and was used on occasion by Mary, Queen of Scots. It was

abandoned to its picturesque decay in the mid-eighteenth century, and today the peaceful ruins and their adjoining grassy lawns make for a great place to explore, with kids in particular loving the run of their very own castle.

Royal Observatory

Blackford Hill, Blackford Hill
☎0131/668 8100, ⊛www.roe.ac.uk.
Bus #41 from George IV Bridge.
Incorporating a house for the Astronomer Royal for Scotland as well as a beautiful library and a university department, the Royal Observatory remains an important international centre for research, some of which involves the remote operation of telescopes in Australia and Hawaii. It isn't generally open to the public other than for

the occasional talk or open day as well as its Friday evening stargazing sessions (usually 7.30–8.30pm; £3.50), when you can make use of the solar and astronomical telescopes and learn a bit more about the night sky. Nonetheless, the building makes an impressive contribution to the profile of Blackford Hill, another of the prime viewpoints on the south side of Edinburgh. The long, dark evenings of winter are the best time to join one of the public sessions, though in summer there's a chance to hunt for sun spots or the Northern Lights.

Hermitage of Braid

Hermitage Drive, Braid Hills ⊛www .cecrangerservice.demon.co.uk. Visitor centre Mon–Thurs & Sun noon–5pm, Fri noon–4pm. Free. Bus #11 or #16 from Lothian Rd. At the foot of Blackford Hill, the bird sanctuary of Blackford Pond is the starting point for one of the many trails running through the Hermitage of Braid nature reserve, a lovely shady area along the course of the Braid Burn, after which it is named, which offers some quiet waterside walks. The castellated eighteenth-century mansion on the burn's bank now serves as a visitor centre; it's mostly aimed at school groups, but you can get some background information on the trails, trees, plants and local wildlife. Immediately to the south are the Braid Hills, most which are occupied by two golf courses which are closed on alternate Sundays in order to allow access for walkers.

The Pentland Hills

Hillend: buses #4 and #15 from Princes St; Flotterstone: McEwans coach #100 from Lothian Rd. Dominating most views of south Edinburgh, the Pentland Hills are an elevated chain, some eighteen miles long and five miles wide, which offer walkers and mountain bikers a thrilling taste of wild Scottish countryside just a few miles beyond the city suburbs. Numerous bike trails and walks, from gentle strolls along well-

▼HIGHLAND CATTLE, PRESTONFIELD HOTEL GROUNDS

▲HIKERS IN THE PENTLAND HILLS

Rosslyn Chapel

Roslin ☎ 0131/440 2159, ◉ www
.rosslyn-chapel
.com. Mon–Sat
10am–5pm, Sun
noon–4.45pm.
£5.50. Lothian Buses
#15A (Mon–Fri) or
First Edinburgh #141
(Sat) from St Andrew
Square. Seven
miles south of
Edinburgh's
centre, tranquil
Roslin has two
unusual claims to
fame: the world's
first cloned
sheep, Dolly,
was created here
at the Roslin
Institute in 1997,
and the village
also boasts the
mysterious,
richly decorated
late-Gothic Rosslyn Chapel.
The latter was intended to
be a huge collegiate church
dedicated to St Matthew, but
construction halted soon after
the founder's death in 1484, and
the vestry built onto the facade
nearly four hundred years later
is the sole subsequent addition.
After a long period of neglect,
a massive restoration project has
recently been undertaken, with
a rigid canopy constructed over
the chapel in order to dry out
the saturated ceiling and walls.
Visitors are free to look around
both inside and out: Rosslyn's
exterior bristles with pinnacles,
gargoyles, flying buttresses
and canopies, while inside
the stonework is, if anything,
even more intricate. The
foliage carving is particularly
outstanding, with botanically
accurate depictions of over
a dozen different leaves and

marked paths to a ten-mile
traverse of the hills and moors,
are outlined in a free pamphlet
available from the Regional
Park Information Centre at
Flotterstone, a former staging
post ten miles south of the
city centre on the A702. The
simplest way to get a taste of
the scenery of the Pentlands is
to set off from the car park by
the ski centre at Hillend at the
northeast end of the range; take
the path up the right-hand side
of the dry ski slopes, turning
left shortly after crossing a stile
to reach a prominent point
with outstanding views over
Edinburgh and Fife. If you're
feeling energetic, the views
get even better higher up, and
you'll get more of an idea of
the unexpected green emptiness
of the Pentland range running
away to the south.

plants. Among them are cacti and Indian corn, compounding the legend that the founder's grandfather, the daring sea adventurer Prince Henry of Orkney, did indeed set foot in the New World a century before Columbus. The greatest and most original carving of all is the extraordinary knotted Apprentice Pillar; it's said to have been made by an apprentice during the absence of the master mason, who killed him in a fit of jealousy on seeing the finished work. The imagery of the carvings around the chapel, together with the history of the family which owns it, the St Clairs of Rosslyn, leave little doubt about its links to the Knights Templar and freemasonry; the chapel is also regularly drawn into conspiracy theories on these themes, appearing as a key link in books such as Dan Brown's recent best-seller *The Da Vinci Code*.

▼ROSSLYN CHAPEL

Scottish Mining Museum

Lady Victoria Colliery, Newtongrange ☏0131/663 7519, ⦿www .scottishminingmuseum.org. Daily: Feb–Oct 10am–5pm; Nov–Jan 10am–4pm. £4.95. Lothian Buses #3A and #29 from Princes St or North Bridge, or First Edinburgh #86 from North Bridge and #95 from St Andrew Square. This industrial heritage museum dedicated to the many collieries found in this area of Scotland is a particularly enjoyable place for kids, its mine and the local community brought to life via "magic helmets" – essentially remote control headphones – which allow you to follow the progress of a shift arriving at the mine and get a taste of the slightly surreal life below ground. Ex-miners now work as tour guides, explaining the origins of coal, what went on at the pithead above the 1625-foot shaft, and the Victorian winding tower, still in working order, which is powered by Scotland's largest steam engine.

Cafés

Kaffe Politik

146 Marchmont Rd, Marchmont ☏0131/446 9873. Closed Sun evening. Café culture hits the student fiefdom of deepest Marchmont, in a relaxed and stylish venue serving coffees and impressive lunchtime and evening light meals such as toasted focaccia and creamy chicken laksa.

S. Luca

16 Morningside Rd, Morningside ☏0131/446 0233, ⦿www.s-luca .co.uk. Family-oriented city outlet for this much loved ice-cream maker from Musselburgh, whose 100-year old recipe doesn't use much more than double cream, milk and butter,

and is made freshly every day. You could also try Irn Bru-flavoured sorbet (or the original drink, of course), knickerbocker glories, simple pasta dishes and panini, all served until 10pm every night.

Restaurants

The Apartment

7–13 Barclay Place (Bruntsfield Place), Bruntsfield ⊕0131/228 6456. Closed Mon–Fri lunch. Hugely popular, highly fashionable modern diner, with IKEA furniture, sisal flooring and abstract modern art on the walls. Their "Chunky, Healthy Lines" feature filling kebabs of meat, fish or vegetables.

The New Bell

233 Causewayside, Newington ⊕0131/668 2868, ⊛www.thenewbell .com. A cosy, pleasant restaurant located above a pub, serving tasty meat and fish dishes that are streets ahead of standard pub fare. Mains such as seared tuna or roast guinea fowl are under £15, and they're followed by crowd-pleasing desserts such as banana tarte tatin.

Sweet Melinda's

11 Roseneath St, Marchmont ⊕0131/229 7953. Closed Sun & Mon lunch. A smart seafood restaurant in a single, timber-panelled room with a friendly neighbourhood feel. It's edging towards the expensive side, but it's worth shelling out for dishes such as mackerel served with chorizo, or beautifully fried squid.

Thaisanuk

21 Argyle Place ⊕0131/228 8855. Dinner only. Tiny diner offering inexpensive sit-in meals as well as some of the best takeaway around. There are dishes from Malaysia and Vietnam alongside the Thai classics, but clean, rich, authentic flavours prevail, and you can bring your own alcohol to help keep the costs down.

Pubs and bars

Human Be-In

2–8 West Crosscauseway, Newington ⊕0131/662 8860, ⊛www.humanbe-in .co.uk. Daily noon–1am. One of Edinburgh's trendiest student bars, with huge plate glass windows to admire the beautiful people, and tables outside for summer posing. Good food, too.

The Canny Man's

239 Morningside Rd, Morningside ⊕0131/447 1484. Mon–Wed 11.30am–11pm, Thurs–Sat 11.30am–midnight, Sun 12.30–11pm. Atmospheric and idiosyncratic pub-cum-museum adorned with anything that can be hung on the walls or from the ceiling. Local ales and over 200 whiskies on offer, as well as snacks.

Golf Tavern

30–31 Wrights Houses, Bruntsfield Links. Daily 10am–1am. A recently made-over bar with a golf theme, set in what's actually quite a historic local tavern. The photos of Ernie Els seem a bit out of place beside the cool chocolate-brown sofas, but you can sit outside and watch the pitch-and-putt golf, with Arthur's Seat as the backdrop.

South Queensferry and the Forth Bridges

The famous Forth Rail Bridge is commonly regarded as an icon of Edinburgh, despite the fact that it's actually located eight miles northwest of the city centre over the narrowest point of the Firth of Forth, the estuary of the Forth river which rises in central Scotland and flows out to the North Sea. At the southern end of the bridge is the historic town of South Queensferry which, despite the drone of traffic passing over the road bridge, is an extremely pleasant spot on the water's edge. It serves as the focal point for visiting the local attractions, which include two grand stately houses and a wonderful ruined abbey on Inchcolm island.

South Queensferry

Named for the saintly wife of king Malcolm Canmore, Margaret, whose chapel sits at the highest point of Edinburgh Castle, South Queensferry is a great place for a wander, with the firth on one side and a palpably historic air. The narrow, cobbled High Street is lined with tightly packed, brightly painted old buildings with pantile roofs, most of which date from the seventeenth and eighteenth centuries. The most dramatic is a black-harled, step-gabled house known as the Black Castle, built in 1626 for a sea captain; on either side of

▼SOUTH QUEENSFERRY

Getting to South Queensferry

It's relatively easy to get to South Queensferry by public transport. Bus #43 operated by First Edinburgh runs frequently from Princes Street or Charlotte Square to South Queensferry, while all trains to Dunfermline, Kirkcaldy and Dundee from central Edinburgh stop at Dalmeny station, from where there's a long flight of steps down to Hawes Pier or a well-signposted half-mile walk to the centre of town. For a scenic alternative, stay on the train across the Forth Rail Bridge, alight at North Queensferry station, work your way across the top of the village to join the footpath over the Forth Road Bridge, and follow this all the way back over the Forth to South Queensferry.

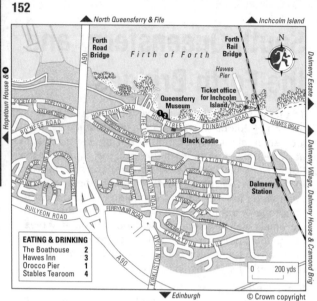

North Queensferry & Fife

Inchcolm Island

Forth
Road
Bridge

Firth of Forth

Forth
Rail
Bridge

Hawes
Pier

Queensferry
Museum

Ticket office
for Inchcolm
Island

HIGH STREET
EDINBURGH ROAD

HAWES BRAE

Black Castle

Dalmeny
Station

HOPETOUN ROAD

BO'NESS ROAD

KIRKLISTON ROAD

FERRYMUIR ROAD

BUILYEON ROAD

A90

Edinburgh

© Crown copyright

EATING & DRINKING

The Boathouse	2
Hawes Inn	3
Orocco Pier	1
Stables Tearoom	4

0   200 yds

South Queensferry and the Forth Bridges — PLACES

Hopetoun House & 1 4

Dalmeny Estate ►

Dalmeny Village, Dalmeny House & Cramond Brig

this the south side of the street has a two-tier arrangement, with arcaded shops below and a walkway for the upper houses running along the top of the shops. Only one row of houses separates the High Street from the water; through the gaps between these there's a great perspective of the two Forth bridges, an old stone harbour and a curved, pebbly beach, the scene each New Year's Day of the teeth-chattering "Loony Dook" (see p.180), when a gaggle of hung-over locals (along with some foolhardy tourists) charge into the sea for the quickest of dips.

Queensferry Museum

High St, South Queensferry ☎0131/331 5545, ⊛www.cac.org.uk. Mon & Thurs–Sat 10am–1pm & 2.15–5pm, Sun noon–5pm. Free. In the rather mundane setting of four upper-floor rooms of council offices, this charming collection of local history and artefacts is worth seeking out just to find out

more about the Burry Man, a bizarre ceremony which takes place in Queensferry every August in which a local man is covered from head to toe in burrs (the spiky seed cases of the burdock plant), then walked around the streets to ward off evil spirits. In a room on the seaward side of the building there's also a big bay window with binoculars and telescopes provided for those who want to give bridges, boats and birds a closer inspection, while nearby boards provide some background on how the mighty Forth bridges were built.

Dalmeny House

Dalmeny Estate, South Queensferry ☎0131/331 1888, ⊛www.dalmeny .co.uk. July & Aug Mon, Tues & Sun 2–5.30pm. £5. Set on a 2000-acre estate between Cramond and South Queensferry, Dalmeny House is not, in truth, the prettiest country seat you'll encounter in Scotland, its Tudor-Gothic style giving rather too much prominence to castellations, towers and chimney stacks. As it's the seat and residence of the Earl of Rosebery, entry is quite restrictive, with viewing via tours only (generally on the hour and half-hour), but the quality of the items on show combined with the intriguing history of the family make it a fascinating place to visit. The fifth earl (1847–1929), a nineteenth-century British Prime Minister, married the heiress Hannah de Rothschild, and their union is the principal reason why Dalmeny boasts some of the finest baroque and Neoclassical furniture produced for Louis XIV, XV and XVI during the hundred years before the French Revolution. Also in the collection are a very rare set of tapestries made from cartoons by Goya, and portraits by Raeburn, Reynolds, Gainsborough and Lawrence as well as a valuable collection of memorabilia relating to Napoleon Bonaparte, who clearly fascinated the fifth Earl – the collection includes the desk Napoleon used on St Helena, and his ornate shaving stand.

Hopetoun House

South Queensferry ☎0131/331 2451, ⊛www.hopetounhouse.com. April–Sept daily 10am–5.30pm. £6.50. Sitting in its own extensive estate on the south shore of the Forth, just to the west of South Queensferry, Hopetoun House ranks as one of the most impressive stately homes in Scotland. The original house was built at the turn of the eighteenth century for the first Earl of Hopetoun by Sir William Bruce, the architect of Holyroodhouse. A couple of decades later, William Adam carried out an

▲ SERVANTS' BELLS, HOPETOUN HOUSE

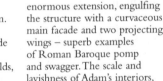

enormous extension, engulfing the structure with a curvaceous main facade and two projecting wings – superb examples of Roman Baroque pomp and swagger. The scale and lavishness of Adam's interiors, most of whose decoration was carried out by his sons after the architect's death, make for a stark contrast with the intimacy of those designed by Bruce – the Red and Yellow Drawing Rooms, with their splendid ceilings by the young Robert Adam, are particularly impressive. Hopetoun's architecture is undoubtedly its most compelling feature, but the furnishings aren't completely overwhelmed, with some impressive seventeenth-century tapestries, Meissen porcelain, and a distinguished collection of paintings, including portraits by Gainsborough, Ramsay and Raeburn. The house's grounds are equally splendid, with a long, regal driveway and lovely walks along woodland trails and the banks of the Forth, as well as plenty of places for a picnic.

▲ FORTH RAIL BRIDGE

The Forth Bridges

Dominating South Queensferry and this section of the Forth are the two mighty, if contrasting, bridges across the water here. The more compelling is the formidable Rail Bridge, built from 1883 to 1890, which ranks among the supreme achievements of Victorian engineering. Plans for a suspension bridge to carry the railway line were ripped up in 1879 when the collapse of the Tay Rail Bridge, with the loss of around 100 lives, demanded some serious rethinking. The revised plans by Sir John Fowler and Benjamin Baker created a cantilevered structure over twice as strong as it actually needed to be. Some 50,000 tons of steel were used in the construction of a design that manages to express grace as well as might: the great French engineer Alexandre-Gustave Eiffel described it as "the greatest wonder of the century", although the artist William Morris did opine that it was "the supremest specimen of all ugliness". Less than half a mile to the west is the parallel and rather more prosaic Road Bridge, whose suspension format was derived from American models such as the Golden Gate Bridge. Completed in 1964, the road bridge finally killed off the 900-year-old ferry, and there's now a sufficiently heavy volume of traffic to prompt talk of the need for a second bridge. The only way to cross the rail bridge is aboard a train heading to or from Edinburgh, though inevitably this doesn't allow much of a perspective of the spectacle itself. For the best panorama, make use of the pedestrian and cycle lane on the east side of the road bridge. You can get some background on both bridges at the South Queensferry Museum (see above), while the Forth Bridges Exhibition (daily 9am–9pm; free), in the *Queensferry Lodge Hotel* on the north side of the road bridge, reveals such various mind-boggling statistics as the number of rivets in the rail bridge (six and a half million), and that a shower of rain adds around 100 tons to its weight.

Inchcolm Island

☎ 01383/823 332, ⊛ www.historic -scotland.gov.uk. Maid of the Forth ☎ 0131/331 4857, ⊛ www .maidoftheforth.co.uk. July–Aug 1–3 trips daily; April–June & Sept–Oct weekends and selected days only. £11.50 (includes admission to the abbey). Some five miles northeast of South Queensferry and reachable via a half-hour boat trips which depart from Hawes Pier at South Queensferry, Inchcolm is the most intriguing and attractive island in the Firth of Forth. The primary draw is the chance to explore the island's abbey, the best-preserved medieval monastic complex in Scotland, although the hour-and-a-half you're given ashore by the boat timetables also allows time for a picnic on the abbey's lawns or the chance to explore Inchcolm's old military fortifications and its extensive bird-nesting grounds. The abbey was founded in 1235 after King Alexander I was stormbound on the island and took refuge in a hermit's cell, and an order of Augustinian monks lived here until the abbey's religious function was curtailed by the Reformation in 1560. The structure as a whole is half-ruined today, but the explorable cluster of buildings include an intact tower, octagonal chapterhouse and echoing cloisters; from different parts of the abbey, tiny windows offer unexpected glimpses of the sea with Edinburgh's distinctive

skyline in the distance. Aside from the abbey, Inchcolm also offers some short walks along paths which crisscross the island, some of which take you past the old installations that are the sole legacy of Inchcolm's one-time incarnation as a military base – gun emplacements, lookout posts and storehouses from both world wars still stand. The paths also afford some attractive views of the Firth, as well as the chance to see some of the island's principal inhabitants, birds – terns, oystercatchers, snipe, kittiwake and raucous gull all nest here at various times in the year. Seals can often be seen basking on the tidal reefs offshore and if you're lucky, you'll see dolphins and porpoises from the boat crossing to the island.

Cafés

Stables Tearoom
Hopetoun House, South Queensferry ☏ 0131/331 3661. April–Sept daily 10am–5.30pm. Classy lunches and afternoon teas with waitress service, even if it is located in

▼INCHCOLM FERRY BOARD

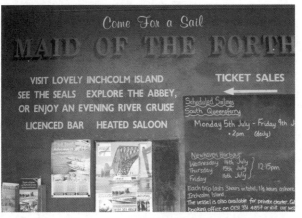

the place where the horses used to get their nosebags.

Restaurants

The Boathouse
19b High St, South Queensferry
☎0131/331 5429. Closed Mon. Not easy to find, as it's so close to the high tide mark that you have to climb down steps to the beach to reach it. The cosy restaurant enjoys great views out to the bridges; the seafaring theme is continued through the menu, which is dominated by moderately expensive but classy seafood, much of it local.

Orocco Pier
17 High St, South Queensferry
☎0131/331 1298, ⊕www.oroccopier
.co.uk. The presence of a style bar in South Queensferry may seem a bit incongruous, but this new place has wowed everyone with its great setting looking out to the bridges, slick contemporary style and moderately priced bistro food, which ranges from steaks to Thai-style mussels.

Pubs and bars

Hawes Inn
Newhalls Rd, South Queensferry
☎0131/331 1990. Mon–Sat 11am–11pm, Sun 12.30–10.30pm. An old wayfarers' inn most famously visited by Robert Louis Stevenson, who used it in his adventure story *Kidnapped*. Now run by a national chain, there's a predictability to the fare and interior style, but its location is a classic spot at the head of a jetty right underneath the Rail Bridge.

▲BOATHOUSE RESTAURANT

Accommodation

Hotels, guesthouses and B&Bs

As befits its status as a busy tourist city and important commercial centre, Edinburgh has a greater choice of accommodation than any other place in Britain outside London. **Hotels** (and large backpacker hostels; see p.167) are essentially the only options you'll find right in the heart of the city, but within relatively easy reach the selection of **guesthouses**, **B&Bs** and **campus accommodation** broadens considerably. **Prices** here are significantly higher than elsewhere in Scotland, with double rooms starting at £60 per night. Budget hotel chains offer the best value if you want basic accommodation right in the centre, with rooms available for £60–80; £80–100 per night will get you something more interesting and stylish. Note that many guesthouses and small hotels are located in Georgian or Victorian townhouses, most of which have three or more floors and no lift and so are not ideal if stairs are a problem. Bear in mind also that advance **reservations** are worthwhile at any time and very strongly recommended for stays during the Festival and around Hogmanay. The Scottish tourist board operates a central booking centre for accommodation all over the country, including Edinburgh; call ☎0845 2255121 or visit ⊛www.visitscotland.com. There's a £3 fee for this service, waived if you book online.

The Royal Mile

Bank Hotel 1 South Bridge ☎0131/622 6800, ⊛www.festival-inns.co.uk. Notable location in a 1920s bank at the crossroads of the Royal Mile and South Bridge, with *Logie Baird's* bar downstairs and nine unusual but comfortable rooms upstairs on the theme of famous Scots. Doubles from £80.

Ibis Edinburgh Centre 6 Hunter Square ☎0131/240 7000, ⊛www.accorhotels. com. Probably the best-located chain hotel cheapie in the Old Town, within sight of the Royal Mile; rooms are modern and inexpensive, but there are few facilities other than a plain bar. Doubles from £75.

Gladstone's Land 477b Lawnmarket, c/o National Trust for Scotland, 5 Charlotte Square ☎0131/243 9331, ⊛www.nts .org.uk. Two classic Old Town apartments on the fourth floor of the historic Gladstone's Land (see p.71). Set up for self-catering, both sleep two in twin beds, and there's a minimum stay of three nights. £435 per week.

The Scotsman Hotel 20 North Bridge ☎0131/556 5565, ⊛www .thescotsmanhotel.co.uk. This plush, smart but non-stuffy new occupant of the grand old offices of the Scotsman newspaper is one of Edinburgh's headline hotels. It's five-star stuff with modern gadgets and fittings, but the marble staircase and walnut panelled lobby have been retained, and you can sleep in the editor's old office. Doubles from £250.

A guide to prices

For hotels, guesthouses and B&Bs, the prices quoted in this chapter are for the cheapest double room in the summer high season, and include breakfast unless otherwise specified. Prices often rise during the Festival and over New Year (Hogmanay). Cheaper rates can sometimes be found if you visit outside high season, book online or book at the last minute. For hostels, we've given the standard price of a dorm bed in high season, as well as the cost of a private (double or twin) room, where available; neither rate includes breakfast.

Travelodge Edinburgh Central 33 St Mary's St ☎0870/191 1637, ®www .travelodge.co.uk. There's more than a hint of concrete brutalism about the look of this chain hotel, but it's well-priced, and well located, 100 yards from the Royal Mile

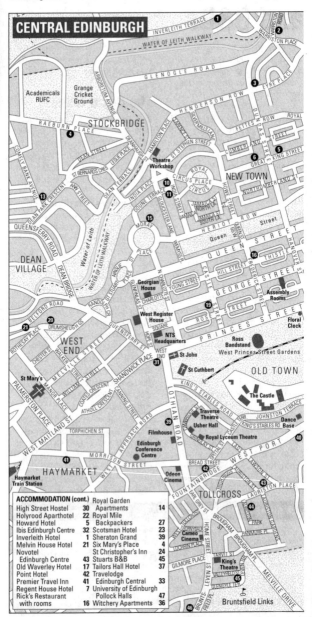

CENTRAL EDINBURGH

ACCOMMODATION (cont.)		Royal Garden	
High Street Hostel	30	Apartments	14
Holyrood Aparthotel	22	Royal Mile	
Howard Hotel	5	Backpackers	27
Ibis Edinburgh Centre	1	Scotsman Hotel	23
Inverleith Hotel		Sheraton Grand	39
Melvin House Hotel	21	Six Mary's Place	4
Novotel		St Christopher's Inn	24
Edinburgh Centre	43	Stuarts B&B	45
Old Waverley Hotel		Tailors Hall Hotel	37
Point Hotel	42	Travelodge	
Premier Travel Inn	41	Edinburgh Central	33
Regent House Hotel	7	University of Edinburgh	
Rick's Restaurant		Pollock Halls	47
with rooms	16	Witchery Apartments	36

opposite a clutch of decent restaurants. Doubles from £70, breakfast not included. **The Witchery Apartments Castlehill**

☎0131/225 5613, ⓦwww.thewitchery.com. Seven riotously indulgent suites grouped around this famously spooky res-

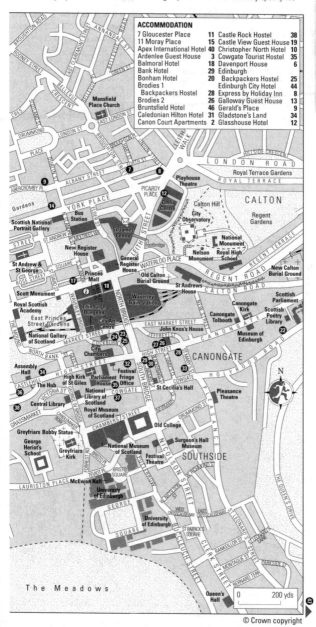

ACCOMMODATION

7 Gloucester Place	11	Castle Rock Hostel	38
11 Moray Place	15	Castle View Guest House	19
Apex International Hotel	40	Christopher North Hotel	10
Ardenlee Guest House	3	Cowgate Tourist Hostel	35
Balmoral Hotel	18	Davenport House	6
Bank Hotel	29	Edinburgh	
Bonham Hotel	20	Backpackers Hostel	25
Brodies 1		Edinburgh City Hotel	44
Backpackers Hostel	28	Express by Holiday Inn	8
Brodies 2	26	Galloway Guest House	13
Bruntsfield Hotel	46	Gerald's Place	9
Caledonian Hilton Hotel	31	Gladstone's Land	34
Canon Court Apartments	2	Glasshouse Hotel	12

© Crown copyright

taurant just downhill from the castle; expect strange antiques, big leather armchairs, tapestry-draped beds, oak panelling and huge roll-top baths, as well as ultra-modern sound systems and complimentary bottles of champagne. Top of the range, unique and memorable. Suites from £275.

Holyrood and Arthur's Seat

Holyrood Aparthotel Nether Bakehouse Close, Holyrood ☎0131/524 3200, ⊛www .holyroodaparthotel.com. A block of two-

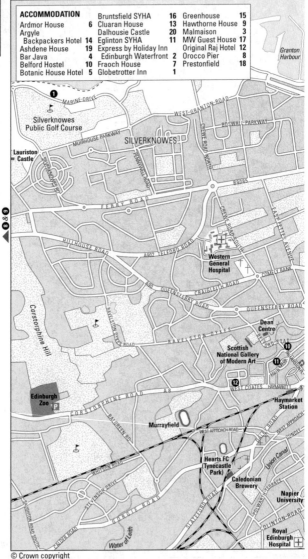

ACCOMMODATION					
Ardmor House	6	Bruntsfield SYHA	16	Greenhouse	15
Argyle		Cluaran House	13	Hawthorne House	9
Backpackers Hotel	14	Dalhousie Castle	20	Malmaison	3
Ashdene House	19	Eglinton SYHA	11	MW Guest House	17
Bar Java	4	Express by Holiday Inn		Original Raj Hotel	12
Belford Hostel	10	Edinburgh Waterfront	2	Orocco Pier	8
Botanic House Hotel	5	Fraoch House	7	Prestonfield	18
		Globetrotter Inn	1		

© Crown copyright

bedroom self-catering apartments near the new Scottish Parliament. The location has lots of Old Town atmosphere, and the accommodation is slick and modern with most mod-cons. Apartments from £120 (two people sharing).

University of Edinburgh Pollock Halls of Residence 18 Holyrood Park Rd, Newington ☎0131/651 2007, ☻www .edinburghfirst.com. Unquestionably the best setting of any of the city's university accommodation, right beside the Royal Commonwealth Pool and Holyrood Park, and with

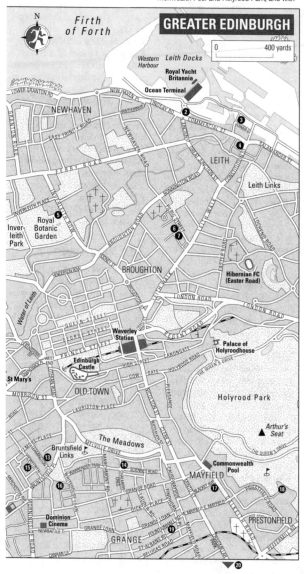

a range of accommodation from single rooms (£28), twins (£56) and en-suite doubles (£72) to self-catering flats (from £350 per week). Available Easter and June to mid-Sept only.

South of the Royal Mile

Apex International Hotel 31–35 Grassmarket ☎0845/608 3456, ☞www .apexhotels.co.uk. This ex-university building turned 175-bed business-oriented hotel has better-than-average rooms, some with views to the Castle. The street-level *Metro* brasserie looks out through plate glass windows onto the happening Grassmarket. Doubles from £90.
Novotel Edinburgh Centre 80 Lauriston Place ☎0131/656 3500, ☞www .accorhotels.com. One of Edinburgh's more stylishly designed chain hotels; not far from the Grassmarket and theatre district, and with a small gym, indoor pool, bar and restaurant. Doubles from £129, breakfast not included.
Point Hotel 34–59 Bread St ☎0131/221 5555, ☞www.point-hotel.co.uk. Treated to a radical contemporary makeover, this former department store is now one of Edinburgh's most stylish and individual modern hotels. There's a popular cocktail bar and a decent restaurant at street level. Doubles from £100, breakfast not included.
Edinburgh City Hotel 79 Lauriston Place ☎0131/622 7979, ☞www .bestwesternedinburghcity.co.uk. Located near Tollcross and the Meadows, this former maternity hospital is now a reasonably individual and smartish medium-sized hotel. Doubles from £125, breakfast not included.
Sheraton Grand 1 Festival Square ☎0131/229 9131, ☞www.sheraton .com/grandedinburgh. Modern, upmarket hotel notable for its sandstone and glass facade which looks across an open plaza to the castle, and the fact that it's home to the city's best spa (☞www.one-spa.com) – you don't have to be resident to make use of it. Doubles from £170, breakfast not included.
Tailors Hall Hotel 139 Cowgate ☎0131/622 6801, ☞www.festival-inns .co.uk. Stylish and modern en-suite rooms in a recently converted 1621 trades hall and brewery in otherwise dingy Cowgate. It's in the same building as the lively, late-night mock-Gothic *Three Sisters Bar* (and beer garden). Doubles from £80.

Along Princes Street

Balmoral Hotel 1 Princes St ☎0131/556 2414, ☞www.roccofortehotels.com. This elegant Edinburgh landmark is the finest grand hotel in the city, with nearly two hundred rooms, full business facilities, a swimming pool and gym and two highly rated restaurants. Doubles from £115, breakfast not included.
Caledonian Hilton Hotel Corner of Princes St and Lothian Rd ☎0131/222 8888, ☞www.hilton.co.uk. This red-sandstone building lording it over the west end of Princes Street was recently taken over by the Hilton Group, and is undergoing a rolling upgrade programme which should help it make up a bit of the ground lost to its competitors in recent years. Doubles from £150.
Old Waverley Hotel 43 Princes St ☎0131/556 4648, ☞www.oldwaverley .co.uk. This rather old-fashioned and plain grand hotel, ideally placed right across from Waverley Station, has been recently refurbished and offers sweeping city views. Doubles from £150.

The New Town

Ardenlee Guest House 9 Eyre Place ☎0131/556 2838, ☞www .ardenleeguesthouse.com. Welcoming non-smoking guesthouse at the foot of the New Town, with original Victorian features and nine reasonably spacious rooms, including some suitable for families. Doubles from £60.
Castle View Guest House 30 Castle St ☎0131/226 5784, ☞www.castleviewgh .co.uk. A lot of stairs (and no lift), and the castle view is sideways-on (and only from certain rooms), but the eight en-suite rooms are pleasant and include some family-friendly ones, while the location is central, right in the heart of the New Town's shops and restaurants. Doubles from £90.
Christopher North Hotel 6 Gloucester Place ☎0131/225 2720, ☞www .christophernorth.co.uk. Elegant and comfortable townhouse hotel in a typically grand New Town terrace. Decor is modern and dramatic, if a little overwhelming. Doubles from £98.
Davenport House 58 Great King St ☎0131/558 8495, ☞www

.davenport-house.com. This grand, regally decorated guesthouse in an attractive townhouse makes a well-priced and intimate alternative to some of the nearby hotels. Doubles from £85.

Gerald's Place 21b Abercromby Place
⊕0131/558 7017, ⊛www.geraldsplace
.com. A real taste of cultured New Town life at an upmarket but wonderfully hospitable and comfy basement B&B. Doubles from £98.

7 Gloucester Place 7 Gloucester Place
⊕0131/225 2974, ⊛www
.stayinginscotland.com. Elegant, well-cared-for bed and breakfast, with three bedrooms on the upper floor of a Georgian terrace house. The best of the double rooms has graceful garden views and use of a classic 1930s bathroom. Doubles from £80.

Howard Hotel 34 Great King St
⊕0131/623 9303, ⊛www.thehoward
.com. Top-of-the-range yet discreet townhouse hotel, with eighteen exclusive rooms lavishly decorated in grand and refined style. Doubles from £170.

11 Moray Place 11 Moray Place
⊕0131/226 4997, wwww.morayplace
.co.uk. An old-fashioned B&B on a street that ranks as the finest of the New Town's architectural splendours. Rooms are on the upper floors and look either over Moray Place gardens or north to Fife. Doubles from £90.

Rick's Restaurant with Rooms 55a
Frederick St ⊕0131/622 7800, ⊛www
.ricksedinburgh.co.uk. Ten much-sought-after rooms at the back of this popular bar and restaurant; all are beautifully styled and fitted with walnut headboards and top quality fabrics, and look out onto a cobbled lane behind. Doubles from £95.

Royal Garden Apartments York Build-ings, Queen St ⊕0131/625 1234,
⊛www.royal-garden.co.uk. Superbly equipped, comfortable modern one- and two-bedroom serviced apartments very centrally located opposite the National Portrait Gallery. From £155.

Calton Hill and Broughton

Ardmor House 74 Pilrig St, Pilrig
⊕0131/554 4944, ⊛www.ardmorhouse
.com. Victorian townhouse with some lovely

original features combined with smart contemporary decor. Gay-owned, straight-friendly, and located halfway between town and Leith. Doubles from £75.

Express by Holiday Inn Picardy Place,
Broughton ⊕0131/558 2300, ⊛www
.hieedinburgh.co.uk. A great location in an elegant old Georgian tenement near the top of Broughton Street, with 160 rooms featuring neat but predictable chain-hotel decor and facilities. Doubles from £95.

Fraoch House 66 Pilrig St, Pilrig
⊕0131/554 1353, ⊛www.fraochhouse
.com. A relaxing six-bedroom guesthouse with a slick, modern look created by its young owners. It's a ten- to fifteen-minute walk from both Broughton Street and the heart of Leith. Doubles from £80.

The Glasshouse Hotel 2 Greenside
Place, Broughton ⊕0131/525 8200,
⊛www.theetoncollection.com. Cloistered behind the castellated facade of Lady Glenorchy's Church, offering 65 chi-chi rooms with push-button curtains and sliding doors opening onto a huge, lush roof garden scattered with Philippe Starck furniture. Perfect if you're in town for a weekend of flash indulgence. Doubles from £175.

Regent House Hotel 3 Forth St,
Broughton ⊕0131/556 1616, ⊛www
.regenthousehotel.co.uk. A small hotel over four floors which makes up for its lack of glamour with a great location (right in the heart of Broughton on a quiet side-street), and by its practicality, with a number of the rooms useful for groups of 3–5 people. Doubles from £75; large rooms from £30 per person.

Along the Water of Leith

Botanic House Hotel 27 Inverleith Row,
Inverleith ⊕0131/552 2563, ⊛www
.botanichousehotel.com. A small but smart family-run hotel with contemporary, cool decor that nicely echoes the Botanic Garden, which can be seen over the garden wall. There's a cosy but stylish bar in the basement, serving bar food. Doubles from £80.

Canon Court Apartments 20 Canonmills
⊕0131/474 7000, ⊛www.canoncourt
.co.uk. A block of smart, comfortable self-

catering one- and two-bedroom apartments not far from Canonmills Bridge over the Water of Leith at the northern edge of the New Town. Studio apartments from £74 per night.

Galloway Guest House 22 Dean Park Crescent, Stockbridge ☎0131/332 3672, ✉galloway_theclarks@hotmail.com. Friendly family-run option in elegant Stockbridge, within walking distance of the centre. Traditional in style but neat and well priced. Doubles from £50.

Inverleith Hotel 5 Inverleith Terrace, Inverleith ☎0131/556 2745, ⊛www.inverleithhotel.co.uk. Pleasant option near the Botanic Garden, with twelve rooms of various sizes in a Victorian terraced house; all are en-suite and tastefully decorated with wooden floors, antiques and tapestries. Doubles from £70.

Six Mary's Place Raeburn Place, Stockbridge ☎0131/332 8965, ⊛www.sixmarysplace.co.uk. A collectively run alternative-style guesthouse with eight smart, fresh looking rooms; a no-smoking policy, and excellent home-cooked vegetarian breakfasts served in a sunny conservatory. Doubles from £80.

Leith

Bar Java 48–50 Constitution St ☎0131/553 2020, ⊛www.hotelbarjava.com. Simple but brightly designed rooms above one of Leith's funkiest bars. Great breakfasts served, and food and drink available till late in the bar itself. Doubles from £50.

Express by Holiday Inn Edinburgh Waterfront Britannia Way, Ocean Drive ☎0870/744 2163, ⊛www.hiex-edinburgh.com. Purpose-built budget hotel that's a good mid-price option in the Leith area. It's in walking distance of the best of the local restaurants and the Ocean Terminal shopping centre, and an easy bus ride into town. Doubles from £89.

Malmaison 1 Tower Place ☎0131/468 5000, ⊛www.malmaison.com. Chic, modern hotel set in the grand old Seamen's Hostel just back from the wharfside. Bright, bold original designs in each room, as well as CD players and cable TV. Also has gym, room service, Parisian brasserie and café-bar. Doubles from £100.

North and west Edinburgh

Bonham Hotel 35 Drumsheugh Gardens, West End ☎0131/623 9301, ⊛www.thebonham.com. One of Edinburgh's most stylish modern boutique hotels, cheekily hiding behind a grand West End Victorian façade and offering an interesting mix of fine period and chic contemporary styling throughout. Doubles from £160.

Melvin House Hotel 3 Rothesay Terrace, West End ☎0131/225 5084, ⊛www.melvinhouse.co.uk. One of Edinburgh's grandest Victorian terraced houses, with exquisite internal wood panelling and a galleried library. The rooms are rather less memorable, though some have outstanding views over Dean village and the city skyline. Doubles from £99.

The Original Raj Hotel 6 West Coates, Haymarket ☎0131/346 1333, ⊛www.rajempire.com. Imaginatively conceived and pleasantly executed, this townhouse hotel has seventeen rooms themed on India and the splendour of the Raj. Doubles from £80

Premier Travel Inn Edinburgh City Centre 1 Morrison Link, Haymarket ☎0870/238 3319, ⊛www.travelinn.co.uk. No-frills chain hotel in a fairly mundane location near Haymarket station, about fifteen minutes' walk from Princes Street. Doubles from £63, breakfast not included.

South Edinburgh

Ashdene House 23 Fountainhall Rd, Grange ☎0131/667 6026, ⊛www.ashdenehouse.com. Well-run, environmentally friendly, non-smoking guesthouse in traditional Victorian style, located in the quiet southern suburbs. Doubles from £70.

Bruntsfield Hotel 69 Bruntsfield Place, Bruntsfield ☎0131/229 1393, ⊛www.thebruntsfield.co.uk. Large, comfortable and fairly peaceful hotel, now part of the Best Western group, a mile south of Princes Street overlooking Bruntsfield Links. Doubles from £180.

Cluaran House 47 Leamington Terrace, Viewforth ☎0131/221 0047, ⊛www.cluaran-house-edinburgh.co.uk.

Pleasant non-smoking B&B in a tastefully decorated house with lots of original paintings on the walls. Serves good wholefood breakfasts. Doubles from £70.

Dalhousie Castle Bonnyrigg, Midlothian ☎01875/820153, ⊛www.dalhousiecastle .co.uk. If you want a stay in a romantic Scottish castle, this is it. Located in rolling countryside about twenty minutes' drive south of the city centre, you'll find luxurious rooms, four-poster beds, log fires, suits of armour and a modern spa behind the thirteenth-century stone walls. Double rooms from £155 in a separate lodge, or £195 in the castle.

The Greenhouse 14 Hartington Gardens, Viewforth ☎0131/622 7634, ⊛www .greenhouse-edinburgh.com. A fully vegetarian/vegan guesthouse, right down to the soaps and duvets, though a relaxed rather than right-on atmosphere prevails. The rooms are neat and tastefully furnished, with fresh fruit and flowers in each. Doubles from £70.

MW Guest House 94 Dalkeith Rd, Newington ☎0131/662 9265, ⊛www .mwguesthouse.co.uk. One of only a few guesthouses in town with fresh, contemporary design. As it's set in a Victorian villa, every room is a bit different: those at the back are a bit quieter. If you're in a car the parking here is easier than some other Southside choices. Doubles from £60.

Prestonfield Priestfield Rd, Prestonfield ☎0131/225 7800, ⊛www.prestonfield .com. This seventeenth-century mansion set in its own park below Arthur's Seat was recently taken over by the *Witchery* team (see p.161), and an extravagant baroque makeover has helped make it one of Edinburgh's most lavish and over-the-top places to stay. Doubles from £195.

The Stuarts B&B 17 Glengyle Terrace, Bruntsfield ☎0131/229 9559, ⊛www .the-stuarts.com. A five-star bed and breakfast, with three comfortable and well-equipped rooms in a basement beside Bruntsfield Links. Doubles from £100.

South Queensferry

Orocco Pier High St ☎0131/331 1298, ⊛www.oroccopier.co.uk. An exciting and stylish alternative to the city centre, set in a historic house on the South Queensferry waterfront. Twelve flash rooms with designer furnishings, cool lighting and electronic mod-cons, as well as a stylish bar and brasserie on site; all have great views out to the Forth Bridges. Doubles from £95.

Hawthorne House 15 West Terrace ☎0131/319 1447, ⊛www .hawthorne-house.com. Simple B&B in a tall, narrow house in the old part of town; the four double or family rooms are all en-suite, and there's a view of the sea and bridges from those at the front, and of the pantile roofs of old South Queensferry from the rear-facing windows. Doubles from £65.

Hostels

Edinburgh is one of the UK's most popular backpacker destinations, and there are a large number of hostels in and around the city centre, ranging in size, atmosphere and quality. Competition is fierce, so be prepared for a bit of enthusiastic marketing when you make an enquiry. For hostels, we provide the standard price of a dorm bed in regular high season, as well as the cost of a private (double or twin) room, where available. You may have to pay a little more for a dorm with fewer beds.

Argyle Backpackers Hotel 14 Argyle Place, Marchmont ☎0131/667 9991, ⊛www.argyle-backpackers.co.uk. Quiet, less intense version of the typical backpackers' hostel, pleasantly located in three adjoining townhouses near the Meadows in studenty Marchmont. The small dorms have single beds, and there's a dozen or so double/twin rooms, as well as a pleasant communal conservatory and garden at the back. Dorms £15; doubles £40.

Belford Hostel 6–8 Douglas Gardens,

West End ☎0131/225 6209, ⊛www
.hoppo.com. Hoppo chain hostel housed in
a converted Arts and Crafts church just west
of the centre, close to the Water of Leith and
the Gallery of Modern Art. Dorms are in box
rooms with the vaulted church ceiling above;
there's also a handful of doubles. The basement communal areas are reasonably varied
and spacious. Dorms £11, doubles £42.

Brodies 1 12 High St, Royal Mile
☎0131/556 6770, ⊛www.brodieshostels
.co.uk. Tucked down a typical Old Town
close, with four fairly straightforward dorms
and limited communal areas. It's smaller
than many hostels, and a little bit more
homely as a result. Dorms £13.50.

Brodies 2 93 High St, Royal Mile
☎0131/556 2223, ⊛www.brodieshostels
.co.uk. The mellow atmosphere at this
smart new hostel is even more marked
than in the sister property across the road.
Smaller dorms as well as doubles and tri-
ples. Dorms £14, doubles £46.50.

Bruntsfield SYHA Hostel 7 Bruntsfield
Crescent ☎0870/004 1114, ⊛www
.syha.org.uk. Overlooking the leafy Bruntsfield Links a mile south of Princes Street,
with accommodation mostly in dorms
– some of these are partially screened-off
"pod rooms" which offer a bit more privacy
and security than standard dorms. Non-
smoking, and Internet access available.
Dorms and pods £14.50.

Castle Rock Hostel 15 Johnston Terrace,
Old Town ☎0131/225 9666, ⊛www
.scotlands-top-hostels.com. Tucked below
the Castle ramparts, with 200 or so beds
arranged in large, bright dorms, as well as
triple and quad rooms and some doubles.
The communal areas include a games room
with pool and ping-pong tables. Dorms £14,
triple and quad rooms £17, doubles £45.

Cowgate Tourist Hostel 94–116 Cowgate,
Old Town ☎0131/226 2153, ⊛www.hos-
telsaccommodation.com. Basic but central
accommodation in small three-, four- and
five-bedroom apartments with kitchens, all
in the heart of the Old Town. Single bed in
apartment £14, twin rooms £34.

Edinburgh Backpackers Hostel 65
Cockburn St, Old Town ☎0131/220
2200, ⊛www.hoppo.com. Very central,
with large but bright dorms and a decent
number of doubles in a tall Old Town build-

ing. The communal areas are pretty standard, though there is a bar and café at street
level. Dorms £13.50, doubles £42.

Eglinton SYHA Hostel 18 Eglinton
Crescent, Haymarket ☎0870/004 1116,
⊛www.syha.org.uk. Situated in a characterful townhouse west of the centre, and
popular amongst groups and families. Dorms
are large, and the communal areas can be
overrun by the groups. Non-smoking, and
Internet access available. Dorms £14.50.

Globetrotter Inn 46 Marine Drive, Cramond ☎0131/336 1030, ⊛www
.globetrotterinns.com. A big departure
from the busy, buzzy city-centre hostels, in
a sylvan parkland setting four miles from
the centre with lovely views of the Firth of
Forth. The 350-plus beds are mostly bunks
with privacy curtains and individual reading
lights, but there are also doubles. There's
access to a gym and sauna, lots of parking
and an hourly shuttle service into town,
as well as regular buses (#42). Families
and kids are not encouraged. Dorms £15,
doubles £42.

High Street Hostel 8 Blackfriars St, Old
Town ☎0131/557 3984, ⊛www
.scotlands-top-hostels.com. Lively and
popular hostel in an attractive sixteenth-
century building just off the Royal Mile.
There are only dorms here, but good communal facilities, which are shared by those
staying at the *Royal Mile Backpackers* just
up the road. Dorms £14.

Royal Mile Backpackers 105 High St,
Old Town ☎0131/557 6120, ⊛www
.scotlands-top-hostels.com. Smallish
hostel popular with longer-term residents.
The communal areas here are very limited,
but guests have use of to the facilities in
nearby sister hostels. Dorms £14.

St Christopher's Inn 9–13 Market St,
Old Town ☎0131/226 1446, ⊛www
.st-christophers.co.uk. Huge and a little
corporate but very much in the modern
hostel style – dorms are of varying size,
and have en-suite bathrooms; some have
TVs and there are a few double rooms.
There's a small communal area but no
kitchen; the ground-floor bar serves food,
though it has more of a reputation for its
noisy party atmosphere and screenings of
antipodean rugby games. Dorms from £15,
doubles £50.

elements such as top-grade theatre, ballet, dance and classical music were gradually introduced, and it's still very much a highbrow event, with forays into populist territory rare. The festival generally runs over the second two weeks of August and the first week of September, and attracts truly international stars alongside some of the world's finest orchestras and opera, theatre and ballet companies. The most popular single event is the dramatic **Fireworks Concert**, held late at night on the final Sunday: the Scottish Chamber Orchestra belts out pop classics from the Ross Bandstand in Princes Street Gardens, accompanied by a spectacular pyrotechnic display high up above the ramparts of the Castle. Unless you want a seat right by the orchestra you don't need a ticket for this event: hundreds of thousands of people view the display from various vantage points throughout the city, the prime spots being Princes Street, Northbridge, Calton Hill or Inverleith Park and the Botanic Gardens by Stockbridge.

Otherwise, **performances** take place at the city's larger venues such as the Usher Hall and the Festival Theatre and, while **ticket prices** run to over £40, it is possible to see shows for £10 or less if you're prepared to queue for the handful of seats sold on the day. The International Festival's headquarters are at The Hub (see p.71); you can contact them for further information, including the annual programme, which is released in April.

The Edinburgh Festival Fringe

Even standing alone from its sister festivals, the **Edinburgh Festival Fringe**, which runs over the final three weeks of August, is a monumental arts gathering – each year it sees over 15,000 performances from 700-plus companies, and features some 12,000 participants from all over the world. There are around 1500 shows every day, round the clock, in 200 venues around the city. While the headlining names at the International Festival reinforce the Festival's cultural credibility as a whole, it is the dynamism, spontaneity and sheer exuberance of the Fringe which dominates Edinburgh every August, giving the city its unique atmosphere. Crucially, because no artistic control is imposed on those who want to produce a show as part of the Fringe, the productions range from the inspired to the diabolical; there's also a highly competitive atmosphere in which one bad review in a prominent publication means box-office disaster. Many unknowns rely on self-publicity, taking to the streets to perform highlights from their show, or pressing leaflets into the hands of every passer-by.

These days, the most prominent aspect of the Fringe is **comedy**. As well as sell-out audiences and quotable reviews, most of the comedy acts are chasing the Perrier Comedy Award, given to the outstanding up-and-coming stand-up or comedy cabaret, and there's no doubt that the Edinburgh Festival is *the* place to catch new talent before it becomes famous, with debuts made by everyone from Monty Python to Graham Norton over the years. Despite the profile of comedy, however, it's still outweighed in terms of number of shows by the Fringe's **theatre** offerings, with hundreds of brand new works airing alongside offbeat classics and familiar Shakespearean tragedies. The venues are often as imaginative as the shows themselves – play-parks, restaurants and even parked cars have all been used to stage plays. The Fringe also offers fine musicals, dance, children's shows, exhibitions, lectures and music – after years of neglect the latter, in particular, has now expanded significantly, with sub-festivals and venues dedicated to youth orchestras, folk and roots music and indie pop and rock.

The full **Fringe programme** is usually available in June from the Festival Fringe Office (☎ 0131/226 0000, ⓦ www.edfringe.com). Postal and telephone bookings for shows can be made

Fringe venues

In addition to numerous tiny and unexpected auditoriums, the four main Fringe venues are the *Assembly Rooms*, the *Pleasance*, the *Gilded Balloon* and tersely named relative newcomer, *C*. Venue complexes rather than single spaces, the latter three colonize nearby spaces for the duration of the Festival – all are safe bets for decent shows and a bit of starspotting.

The atmosphere at the **Pleasance** is usually less frenetic than at the other venues, with classy drama and whimsical appearances by panellists on Radio 4 game shows. **The Assembly Rooms** provide a grand setting for top-of-the-range drama by companies such as the RSC and big-name music and comedy acts. The Fringe's premier comedy venue, **The Gilded Balloon**, lost its longstanding home in a fire in early 2003, but was up and running in various new venues around town by the time the Festival came along. The disparate locations of **C** have the most varied programme of the big four, and in recent years have been known to stage controversial productions that other venues might be too wary to promote.

While it's nothing like as large as the venues above, you shouldn't ignore the programme put on at the **Traverse Theatre**'s three stages. Long a champion of new drama, the "Trav" combines the avant-garde with slick presentation, and its plays are generally among the Fringe's most acclaimed.

immediately after its release, while during the Festival, tickets are sold at the Fringe Office, on the Royal Mile at no. 180 (daily 10am–9pm), as well as online or at venues. **Ticket prices** for most Fringe shows start at £5, and average from £8 to £12 at the main venues, with the better-known acts going for even more. Although some theatre and music acts can be longer, most performances are scheduled to run for an hour. Performances go on round the clock: if so inclined, you could sit through twenty shows in a day.

Edinburgh International Film Festival

The **Edinburgh International Film Festival** runs for the last two weeks of August, normally finishing at around the same time as the Fringe, and claims a distinguished history at the cutting edge of cinema, premiering American blockbusters from directors like Steven Spielberg and Woody Allen, discovering low-budget smashes such as *My Beautiful Launderette* and the *Blair Witch Project*, and introducing serious contenders such as *East is East*, *Amelie* and *Super Size Me*.

The Film Festival offers the chance to see some of the year's big movies before they go on general release, along with a varied and exciting bill of reissues; for those in the industry, it's also a vital talking shop, with debates, seminars and workshops all spiced up by the attendance of Hollywood stars at the succession of glittering parties which accompany the launches. **Tickets** (£5–10, pre-booking often necessary) and **information** are available from the main venue, the Filmhouse, 88 Lothian Rd, EH3 9BZ ☎0131/228 2688, ⓦwww .edfilmfest.org.uk.

Edinburgh International Book Festival

Launched in 1983, the annual two-week **Edinburgh International Book Festival**, which takes place in the last two weeks of August, is a mammoth celebration of the written word. It's held in a tented village in the genteel setting of Charlotte

Square, and offers talks, readings and signings by a star-studded line-up of visiting authors, as well as panel discussions and workshops. Well-known local writers such as Ian Rankin, A.L. Kennedy and Alexander McCall-Smith make an appearance most years, while visitors from further afield have included Doris Lessing, Louis de Bernières, Ben Okri, John Updike and Vikram Seth. In addition, there are cook-ups by celebrity chefs promoting their latest tomes, and a dedicated programme of children's activities and book-related events.

Tickets (generally £7–8) often sell out quickly, particularly for the big-name events. For tickets and info during the Festival, contact the ticket office at Charlotte Square (☎0131/624 5050, ✆www .edbookfest.co.uk); for **information** before it starts, check the festival website or contact the Scottish Book Centre, 137 Dundee St, EH11 1BG ☎0131/228 5444.

Edinburgh International Jazz and Blues Festival

The **Edinburgh International Jazz and Blues Festival** runs immediately prior to the Fringe in the first week in August, easing the city into the festival spirit with a full programme of gigs in many different locations. Like all the other festivals, this one has grown over the years from a concentrated international summer camp to a bigger, more modern affair, reflecting the panoply of generations and styles which appear under the banner of jazz and blues. Scotland's own varied and vibrant jazz scene is always fully represented, and atmospheric late-night clubs complement major concerts given by international stars. Past visitors have included B.B. King, Bill Wyman, Dizzy Gillespie, Dave Brubeck, Van Morrison, Carol Kidd and the Blues Band, while highlight events include Jazz On A Summer's Day, a musical extravaganza

in Princes Street Gardens, and a colourful New Orleans-style street parade.

The **programme** is available at the end of May from the office at 29 St Stephen's St, EH3 5AN ☎0131/225 2202, ✆www .jazzmusic.co.uk. **Tickets** range in price from £5 for small pub gigs to £20 for a seat in the big venue, and are available from The Hub, Castlehill (☎0131/473 2000, ✆www.hubtickets.co.uk).

The Military Tattoo

Staged in the spectacular stadium of the Edinburgh Castle esplanade, the **Military Tattoo** is an unashamed display of pomp and military pride. The programme of choreographed drills, massed pipe bands, historical tableaux, energetic battle re-enactments, national dancing and pyrotechnics has been a feature of the Festival for fifty years, the emotional climax provided by a lone piper on the Castle battlements. Followed by a quick firework display (longer and more splendid on Saturdays), it's a successful formula barely tampered with over the years.

Tickets (£10–30 depending on seat location) need to be booked well in advance, and it's advisable to take a cushion and rainwear. Both tickets and general **information** are available from the Tattoo Office, 32 Market St, EH1 1QB ☎0131/225 1188, ✆www.edintattoo .co.uk.

The Edinburgh Mela

Held halfway between the New Town and Leith in Pilrig Park over the first weekend in September, the **Edinburgh Mela** coincides with the finale of the International Festival. Truly a people's event, it was introduced in the mid-1990s by the capital's Asian community – the word "Mela" is a Sanskrit term meaning "gathering", and is used to describe many different community events and festivals on the Asian subcontinent. In Edinburgh, the Mela is about cultural diversity, and the family-oriented programme is designed to celebrate the many different cultures in the city. Music, dance, foods, carnivals, fashion shows, sports, children's events, crafts and a two-day careers fair for school-leavers

see the festival season out with a bang rather than a whimper. Further **details** are available from Edinburgh Mela, 14 Forth St ☎0131/557 1400, Ⓦ www. edinburgh-mela.co.uk.

Events calendar

January 1
Loony Dook South Queensferry beach. Free. While most of Edinburgh sleeps off its Hogmanay hangover (see below) a group of hardy locals and over-enthusiastic visitors go for a swim in the Firth of Forth at noon. Join in if you're brave enough, or just look on – and shiver.

January 1–31
Turner Watercolours National Gallery of Scotland (see p.106) ☎0131/624 6200, Ⓦwww.natgalscot.ac.uk. Free. While the light is at its weakest, the gallery's splendid collection of watercolours by J.M.W. Turner is put on display.

January 25
Burns' Night Scots dust down their kilts to celebrate the birthday of Robert Burns, the national bard. Burns Suppers involving haggis, whisky, poetry recitations and songs are traditionally held around this date; if you don't secure an invitation, some are open to the public (check local listings/posters for details), while restaurants put on a special Burns' Night menu.

February/March
Rugby Internationals Murrayfield Stadium (see p.141) ☎0131/346 5000, Ⓦwww.scottishrugby.org. Average ticket price £35. Scotland's rugby union team take on England, Wales, Ireland, France and Italy in the annual Six Nations tournament; in any year, two or three matches will be played in front of 65,000 spectators at Murrayfield Stadium.

April
Science Festival ☎0131/558 7666, Ⓦwww.sciencefestival.co.uk. £4–8 per event. An increasingly high-profile and enterprising Easter festival dedicated to science and technology, offering lots of fun, hands-on events for kids and families, along with newsworthy discussion forums

and more serious lectures.

30 April
Beltane Fire Festival Calton Hill (see p.47). A modern incarnation of the old Celtic festival, celebrating the arrival of spring, which takes place outdoors on the night before May Day – lots of painted naked flesh, troops of beating drums, huge bonfires and plenty of New-Agey symbolism. The event was ticketed for the first time in 2004, but future plans were unconfirmed at the time of writing; contact the tourist office (see p.172) for more information.

late May/early June
Children's Festival ☎0131/225 8050, Ⓦwww.imaginate.org.uk. Tickets £3–5. A sort of mini-Edinburgh Festival for mini folk, with a lively line-up of top-grade children's theatre, puppetry and dance from around the world held at various venues around town.

June
Caledonian Beer Festival Caledonian Brewery (see p.140) ☎0131/337 1286, Ⓦwww.caledonian-brewery.co.uk. £7, including beer vouchers. Edinburgh's last remaining traditional brewery lines up barrels, bands and barbecues for a two-day event showcasing their own excellent beers alongside a leg-wobbling line-up of real ales from around Britain.
Royal Highland Show Royal Highland Showground, Ingliston ☎0131/335 6200, Ⓦwww.royalhighlandshow.org. £16–18. This four-day agricultural fair is Scotland's largest – prize livestock and lots of tractors dominate, but there are also food and craft halls, sheep shearing and show jumping.

July
Pride Scotia ☎0131/556 9471, Ⓦwww .pride-scotia.org. Colourful, high-spirited annual parade and rally staged by Scotland's lesbian, gay and transgender com-

munity. Alternates between Glasgow (even years) and Edinburgh (odd years).

Late July
Jazz and Blues Festival This week-long series of gigs and grooves gets the city in the mood for the Edinburgh Festival. See p.179.

August
Edinburgh Festival The various parts of this mind-boggling festival dominate the capital throughout August. See p.176.

September
Doors Open Day c/o Cockburn Association ☎0131/557 8686, ⊛www .cockburnassociation.org.uk. **Free.** A great opportunity to visit a number of historically and architecturally interesting buildings, most of which are otherwise closed to the public. Venues change each year, but range from private houses to the Central Mosque. Normally takes place on the last Saturday in September.

November
St Andrew's Day Scotland's patron saint is commemorated on 30 November; controversially, it isn't a public holiday, although it is the one day of the year you can get free entrance to Edinburgh Castle.

December
Capital Christmas ⊛www .edinburghscapitalchristmas.org. Of the various seasonal events lined up through December, most prominent is the huge ferris wheel beside the Scott Monument, with an outdoor skating rink installed nearby (see p.105).

December 31
Hogmanay ⊛www.edinburghshogmanay .org. Hogmanay is the Scots' name for New Year's Eve, a unique mix of tradition, hedonism, sentimentality and enthusiasm. Its roots lie in ancient pagan festivities based around the winter solstice, which in most places gradually merged with Christmas; when hardline Scottish Protestant clerics abolished the Catholic mass of Christmas in the sixteenth century, the Scots, not wanting to miss out on a mid-winter knees-up, instead put their energy into greeting the New Year, a tradition which continues to this day. Edinburgh has established a reputation for hosting one of the liveliest parties, with 100,000 people thronging the city centre to enjoy live bands, dancing, plenty of drinking and a massive fireworks display from the castle and other prominent landmarks at midnight. Passes to the street party are free, and are available on a first-come-first-served basis, from early October onwards, from the Hub on Castlehill (☎0131/473 2000) or via the website.

Directory

Airlines British Airways ☎0870/850 9850, ⊛www.ba.com; British European ☎0871/700 0123, ⊛www.flybe.com; British Midland ☎0870/607 0555, ⊛www. flybmi.com; EasyJet ☎0870/600 0000, ⊛www.easyjet.com; KLM ☎0870/507 4074, ⊛www.klm.com.
Banks and exchange All the major UK banks have branches in central Edinburgh, with ATMs and currency exchange; the main concentrations are in the area between Hanover Street and St Andrew Square in the east end of the central New Town. Post offices (see p.178) will exchange currency commission-free; you can also try Thomas Cook, 28 Frederick St (Mon–Sat 9am–5.30pm; ☎0131/465 7700); and currency exchange bureaux in the main tourist office (see p.172). To change money after hours, try one of the upmarket hotels – but expect a hefty commission charge.

Bike rental Although hilly, Edinburgh is a reasonably bike-friendly city with several cycle paths, all of which are detailed on the map published by local cycling action group Spokes (☎0131/313 2114, ⊛www .spokes.org.uk). For rental, try Edinburgh Cycle Hire, just off the Royal Mile at 29 Blackfriars St (☎0131/556 5560; ⊛www .cyclescotland.co.uk; £10–15 per day.
Car rental Arnold Clark, Lochrin Place ☎0131/228 4747; Avis, 5 West Park Place ☎0131/337 6363; Budget, Edinburgh Airport ☎0131/333 1926; Europcar, 24 East London St ☎0131/557 3456; Hertz, 10 Picardy Place ☎0131/556 8311; Thrifty, 42 Haymarket Terrace ☎0131/337 1319.
Car parking It is emphatically not a good idea to take a car into central Edinburgh: despite the presence of several expensive multistorey car parks, finding somewhere to park involves long and often fruitless

searches. Street parking restrictions are draconian: residents' zone parking areas and double-yellow lines are no-go areas at all times, while cars parked for more than five minutes on single yellow lines or overdue parking-meter-controlled areas are likely to be fined £40 by one of the swarms of inspectors who patrol day and night. In severe cases cars can be towed away, with a retrieval fee of £120. Most ticket and parking-meter regulations cease at 6.30pm Monday to Friday, and at 1.30pm on Saturday.

Football Edinburgh's two Premier Division teams normally play at home to passionate crowds of around 10,000 on alternate weekends. Heart of Midlothian currently play at Tynecastle Stadium, Gorgie Road (☎0131/200 7201; ⊛www.heartsfc.co.uk), a couple of miles west of the centre, though it's possible that they'll sell their ground and play home fixtures at nearby Murrayfield rugby stadium (see p.141). Hibernian play at Easter Road Stadium (☎0131/661 1875, ⊛www.hibs.co.uk), a mile northeast of the centre. Match tickets cost around £15.

Gay and lesbian contacts Gay and lesbian switchboard (Mon–Sun 7.30–10pm; ☎0131/556 4049); Edinburgh LGBT Centre for Health and Wellbeing, 9 Howe St (☎0131/523 1100; ⊛www.lgbthealth .org.uk).

Genealogical research General Register Office for Scotland ☎0131/334 0380; ⊛www.scotlandspeople.gov.uk; Scottish Genealogy Society, 15 Victoria Terrace ☎0131/220 3677, ⊛www.scotsgenealogy .com; Scottish Roots, 22 Forth St ☎0131/ 477 8214, ⊛www.scottishroots.com.

Golf Edinburgh is awash with fine golf courses, but most are private. The best public 18-hole courses are the two on the Braid Hills (both on ☎0131/447 6666).

Hospital Edinburgh's new Royal Infirmary at Little France, about four miles southeast of the city centre (☎0131/536 1000), has a 24hr casualty department. There are also casualty departments at the Western General, two miles northwest of the centre on Crewe Road North ☎0131 537 1000 (24hrs), and for children at the Sick Kids' hospital, near the Meadows on Sciennes Road ☎0131 536 0000.

Internet There are plenty of places around Edinburgh where you can go online. Many hotels, guesthouses and hostels have facilities; in the centre of town try Electronic Corner, beside Platform 1 at Waverley Station (Mon–Fri 7.30am–9pm, Sat 8am–9pm, Sun 9am–9pm), or Internet Cafe, 98 West Bow (daily 10am–11pm) at

the east end of the Grassmarket.

Left luggage Counter by platform 1 at Waverley Station (daily 7am–11pm; ☎0131/550 2333).

Lost property Edinburgh Airport ☎0870/040 0007; Edinburgh Police HQ ☎0131/311 3141; Lothian Buses ☎0131/558 8858; First Bus ☎0870/872 7271; Scotrail ☎0141/335 3276.

Money The basic unit of currency in Scotland is the pound sterling (£), divided into 100 pence (p). Bank of England banknotes are legal tender in Scotland; in addition, the Bank of Scotland, the Royal Bank of Scotland and the Clydesdale Bank issue their own banknotes, including the now rare £1 notes. A number of shops and services (but by no means all) will accept payment in euros.

Opening hours Traditional shop hours are Monday to Saturday 9 or 10am to 5.30 or 6pm, but you'll find many of the city centre shops open on Sundays and later on Thursday and/or Friday evenings. The basic licensing hours for pubs are 11am–11pm daily, though most close later on Friday and Saturday nights and open later on Sundays. Restaurants are generally open at lunchtime from noon–2pm and in the evening from 7–10pm, though some are open longer hours or don't shut during the afternoon. The most common days for a restaurant to be closed are Sunday or Monday.

Pharmacy Boots, 48 Shandwick Place (☎0131/225 6757; Mon–Fri 8am–8pm, Sat 8am–6pm, Sun 10.30am–4.30pm).

Police In an emergency call 999. Otherwise contact the Force Communications Centre on ☎0131/311 3131.

Post office The largest post office in central Edinburgh is in the St James Centre at the east end of Princes St (Mon–Sat 9am–5.30pm, closed Sun; ☎0845/722 3344).

Swimming pools Edinburgh has one Olympic-standard modern pool, the Royal Commonwealth, at 21 Dalkeith Rd, Newington (☎0131/667 7211); and some considerably older pools, including Glenogle Road in Stockbridge (☎0131/343 6376); and 6 Thirlestane Rd in Marchmont (☎0131/447 0052). For all opening hours and details of facilities follow the links to "Leisure" at ⊛www.edinburgh.gov.uk.

Tipping There are few fixed rules regarding tipping. Where you've received table service in a restaurant, 10 percent is typical for good service, though you should check that a service charge (often 12.5 percent) hasn't already been added to your bill. You are within your rights to delete this and pay a more appropriate sum.

CLOUDS

ACCOMMODATION AGENCY

THE PERFECT MATCH - EVERYTIME

A HOME FROM HOME!

- STYLISH EDINBURGH FLATS
  (FULLY EQUIPPED – SELF-CATERING)

- SHORT TERM LET SPECIALISTS
  (MINIMUM STAY 4 WEEKS)
- LONG STAY CATERED FOR
  (INDIVIDUALLY TAILORED CONTRACTS)

- PRICES START AT AROUND £1,000 PER MONTH
  (INCLUDING BILLS)

- ALL PROPERTY DETAILS & PHOTOS ON OUR WEBSITE

WWW.CLOUDS.CO.UK

26 FORTH STREET, EDINBURGH EH1 3LH
TEL: 0131-550-3808 · FAX: 0131-550-3807
www.clouds.co.uk · email: info@clouds.co.uk
VAT REG. No. 8041 432 72

small print & Index

A Rough Guide to Rough Guides

Edinburgh DIRECTIONS is published by Rough Guides. The first *Rough Guide to Greece*, published in 1982, was a student scheme that became a publishing phenomenon. The immediate success of the book – with numerous reprints and a Thomas Cook prize short-listing – spawned a series that rapidly covered dozens of destinations. Rough Guides had a ready market among low-budget backpackers, but soon also acquired a much broader and older readership that relished Rough Guides' wit and inquisitiveness as much as their enthusiastic, critical approach. Everyone wants value for money, but not at any price. Rough Guides soon began supplementing the "rougher" information about hostels and low-budget listings with the kind of detail on restaurants and quality hotels that independent-minded visitors on any budget might expect, whether on business in New York or trekking in Thailand. These days the guides offer recommendations from shoestring to luxury and cover a large number of destinations around the globe, including almost every country in the Americas and Europe, more than half of Africa and most of Asia and Australasia. Rough Guides now publish:

- Travel guides to more than 200 worldwide destinations
- Dictionary phrasebooks to 22 major languages
- Maps printed on rip-proof and waterproof Polyart™ paper
- Music guides running the gamut from Opera to Elvis
- Reference books on topics as diverse as the Weather and Shakespeare
- World Music CDs in association with World Music Network

Visit **www.roughguides.com** to see our latest publications.

Publishing information

This 1st edition published June 2005 by
Rough Guides Ltd, 80 Strand, London WC2R 0RL.
345 Hudson St, 4th Floor, New York, NY 10014,
USA.

Distributed by the Penguin Group
Penguin Books Ltd, 80 Strand, London WC2R 0RL
Penguin Group (USA), 375 Hudson Street, NY
10014, USA
Penguin Group (Australia), 250 Camberwell Road,
Camberwell, Victoria 3124, Australia
Penguin Group (Canada), 10 Alcorn Avenue,
Toronto, ON M4V 1E4, Canada
Penguin Group (New Zealand), Cnr Rosedale and
Airborne Roads, Albany, Auckland, New Zealand
Typeset in Bembo and Helvetica to an original
design by Henry Iles.

Printed and bound in China by Leo

© Donald Reid June 2005

No part of this book may be reproduced in any form
without permission from the publisher except for
the quotation of brief passages in reviews.
192pp includes index

A catalogue record for this book is available from
the British Library

ISBN 1-84353-454-1

The publishers and authors have done their best to
ensure the accuracy and currency of all the information in **Edinburgh DIRECTIONS**, however, they
can accept no responsibility for any loss, injury or
inconvenience sustained by any traveller as a result
of information or advice contained in the guide.

1   3   5   7   9   8   6   4   2

O|S Ordnance Survey® This product includes mapping data licensed from Ordnance Survey ®
with the permission of the Controller of Her Majesty's Stationery Office.
© Crown copyright. All rights reserved. Licence No: 100020918.

Help us update

We've gone to a lot of effort to ensure that the first edition of **Edinburgh DIRECTIONS** is accurate and up-to-date. However, things change – places get "discovered", opening hours are notoriously fickle, restaurants and rooms raise prices or lower standards. If you feel we've got it wrong or left something out, we'd like to know, and if you can remember the address, the price, the phone number, so much the better.

We'll credit all contributions, and send a copy of the next edition (or any other DIRECTIONS guide or Rough Guide if you prefer) for the best letters. Everyone who writes to us and isn't already a subscriber will receive a copy of our full-colour thrice-yearly newsletter. Please mark letters: **"Edinburgh DIRECTIONS Update"** and send to: Rough Guides, 80 Strand, London WC2R 0RL, or Rough Guides, 4th Floor, 345 Hudson St, New York, NY 10014. Or send an email to **mail@roughguides.com**

Have your questions answered and tell others about your trip at **www.roughguides.atinfopop.com**

Rough Guide credits

Text editor: Polly Thomas
Layout: Dan May
Photography: Helena Smith
Cartography: Ed Wright
Picture editor: Joe Mee

Proofreader: Ken Bell
Production: Julia Bovis
Design: Henry Iles
Cover design: Chloë Roberts

The author

Donald Reid was brought up in Glasgow, studied law in Edinburgh and left the country soon afterwards to avoid the threat of an office. He saw a bit of the world from the decks of yachts and fishing boats, jumped ship to hang out in Cape Town for a few years and returned to Scotland in the late 1990s to work as a freelance writer and editor.

Acknowledgements

The author would like to express his thanks to Phil Muncaster for sterling work with the guide, as well as Helena for her enthusiasm, ideas and some great images. Polly again proved a great teammate, valued critic and steady edi. There are many around Edinburgh who have helped by opening doors, pointing the way, offering suggestions, providing information and serving coffee – your assistance and support are much appreciated. The biggest contribution of all was from Riona and her mum: two locals who keep me right.

Polly Thomas would like to thank Donald for being a pleasure to work with and for producing a cracking book; Helena for the lovely pictures and for all her help and insider's knowledge; Ed for marvellous maps; and Dan for doing a fab layout job.

Readers' letters

Thanks to all those readers of the Mini Rough Guide to Edinburgh who took the trouble to write in with amendments and suggestions. Apologies for any misspellings or omissions.

Ross and Kathleen Birnie, Pam Buchanan, Diana Campbell, H. Campbell, Tom Corbett, Linda Davis, Robert Dow, James Dress, Alison Duncan, Shirley Eastcott, Matthew Hall, Marion Johns, Lydia Kerr, Ian Marron, Ann McDonald, Martin, Richard Meadows, C. Metcalf, Alex Pattison-Appleton, Ross and Lorna, Mark Rowley, Ed Schlenk, Millicent Scott, Adrian Skivington, Hilary Thacker, Tamara Whitsun and Adrian Wood

Photo credits

All images © Rough Guides except the following:
p.2 Princes Street © Derek Croucher/Corbis
p.4 Military Tattoo at Edinburgh Castle © Jeff J. Mitchell/Reuters/Corbis
p.5 View over Edinburgh with Arthur's Seat in the distance © Credit Line Worldwide Picture Library/Alamy
p.11 Edinburgh Castle © Niall Benvie/Corbis
p.12 Fireworks at the Edinburgh Festival © Peter Turnley/Corbis
p.12 Firework Finale at the Edinburgh Festival © Tony Marsh/Scotsman Publications Ltd
p.13 Jimmy Carr repels hecklers at The Gilded Balloon Teviot © Tom Finnie/ATOM/ePicscotland.com
p.15 Clouet, François (1522-1572) Mary, Queen of Scots (1542-1587) © The Royal Collection © 2004, Her Majesty Queen Elizabeth II.
p.20 Holyrood Abbey © Andrew E. Morse/Alamy
p.21 Inchcolm Castle © Malcolm Fife/Alamy
p.22 Monro Skeleton © Surgeon's Hall Museum
p.28 The Loony Dook © Neil Hanna/The Scotsman Publications Ltd
p.29 Golfers beneath Edinburgh Castle © Adam Woolfitt/Corbis
p.29 Six Nations rugby union match at Murrayfield © Ian Hodgson/Corbis

p.33 National Gallery © David Paterson/Corbis
p.33 Georgian dining room interior © National Trust For Scotland
p.36 The Cadies and Witchery Tours © City of Edinburgh Council/The Cadies and Witchery Tours
p.42 Pride Scotia © Bill Henry/Tony Marsh/Scotsman Publications Ltd
p.43 CC Blooms © Helena Smith
p.46 Hogmanay © Alistair Linford/Stringer/Corbis
p.47 Princes Street Gardens © Graham Knowles/Alamy
p.47 Fire dancers at the Beltane Festival © Corbis
p.47 The Caledonian Beer festival © The Caledonian Brewing Company Ltd
p.47 Clydesdale horse, Royal Highland Show © Kit Houghton/Corbis
p.53 Newtongrange Lothian Wheel, Scottish Mining Museum © Doug Houghton/Alamy
p.57 The Surgeon's Museum © The Surgeon's Museum
p.64 The Forth Bridge © Credit Line David Paterson/Alamy
p.148 Walking in the Pentland Hills © Credit Line StockShot/Alamy

Index

Maps are marked in **colour**

a

accommodation (by area)
Along Princes Street 164
Along the Water of Leith 165
Calton Hill and Broughton 165
Holyrood and Arthur's Seat 162
Leith 166
New Town, The 164
North and west Edinburgh 166
Royal Mile, The 159
South Edinburgh 166
South of the Royal Mile 164
South Queensferry and the Forth Bridges 167
accommodation 159–168
accommodation, Central Edinburgh 160
accommodation, Greater Edinburgh 162
Apex International Hotel 164
Ardenlee Guest House 164
Ardmor House 165
Argyle Backpackers Hotel 167
Ashdene House 166
Balmoral Hotel 164
Bank Hotel 159
Bar Java 166
Belford Hostel 167
Bonham Hotel 166
Botanic House Hotel 165
Brodies 1 168
Brodies 2 168
Bruntsfield Hotel 166
Bruntsfield SYHA Hostel 168
Caledonian Hilton Hotel 164
Canon Court Apartments 165
Castle Rock Hostel 168
Castle View Guest House 164
Christopher North Hotel 164
Cluaran House 166
Cowgate Tourist Hostel 168
Dalhousie Castle 45, 167
Davenport House 164
Edinburgh Backpackers Hostel 168
Edinburgh City Hotel 164
Eglinton SYHA Hostel 168
11 Moray Place 165
Express by Holiday Inn 165
Express by Holiday Inn Edinburgh Waterfront 166
Fraoch House 165
Galloway Guest House 166
Gerald's Place 165
Gladstone's Land 21, 159
The Glasshouse Hotel 165
Globetrotter Inn 168
The Greenhouse 167
Hawthorne House 167
High Street Hostel 168
Holyrood Aparthotel 162
Howard Hotel 165
Ibis Edinburgh Centre 159
Inverleith Hotel 166
Malmaison 135, 137, 166
Melvin House Hotel 166
MW Guest House 167
Novotel Edinburgh Centre 164
Old Waverley Hotel 164
The Original Raj Hotel 166
Orocco Pier 167
Point Hotel 55, 164
Premier Travel Inn Edinburgh City Centre 166
Prestonfield 56, 167
Regent House Hotel 165
Rick's Restaurant with Rooms 165
Royal Garden Apartments 165
Royal Mile Backpackers 168
St Christopher's Inn 168
The Scotsman Hotel 159
Sheraton Grand 45, 164
7 Gloucester Place 165
Six Mary's Place 166
The Stuarts B&B 167
Tailors Hall Hotel 164
Travelodge Edinburgh Central 160
University of Edinburgh Pollock Halls of Residence 163
The Witchery Apartments 45, 161
Adam family of architects 32, 92
Adam, Robert 72, 95, 102, 112, 119, 153
Adam, William 153
Adventure Centre, Ratho 29, 52, 143
airport 171
Almond River 60, 142
anaesthetic, discovery of 111
ancestor research 22, 102, 180
architecture 54
Ardmor House 43, 165
Arthur's Seat 84
Arthur's Seat 8, 28, 49, 82–89

b

B&Bs 159–167
backpacker hostels 167

Balmoral Hotel 104, 108, 109, 164
banks 181
bars see pubs and bars
bed and breakfasts 159–167
beer 47
Beltane Fire Festival 47, 180
bike rental 181
Blackford Hill 146, 147
Bonnar, Joseph 114
Bonnie Prince Charlie 67, 110
Book Festival 178
bookshops 25, 97, 108, 124
Botanic Garden 48, 51, 62, 126, 131
Bourne Fine Art Gallery 114
Braid Hills 147
Brass Rubbing Centre 53, 74
Britannia, Royal Yacht 7, 14, 15, 61, 135
Brodie, Deacon 80
Brodie, Miss Jean 145
Broughton 120
Broughton 7, 42, 119–125
Broughton Street 122
Bruntsfield Links 145
Burke, William 92, 96
Burns, Robert 25, 72, 76, 180
bus tours 172
buses 171
Bute House 112

c

Cadenhead's Whisky Shop 39, 77
cafés (by area)
Along Princes Street 108
Along the Water of Leith 131
Calton Hill and Broughton 124
Holyrood and Arthur's Seat 89
Leith 136
New Town 114
Royal Mile 78
South Edinburgh 149
South of the Royal Mile 98
South Queensferry and the Forth Bridges 155
cafés
Always Sunday 78
Au Gourmand 131
Beanscene 89
Black Medicine Coffee Company 98
Blue Moon Café 43, 124
Bongo Café 89
Café DeLos 98

Café Hub 78
Café Mediterraneo 124
Café Newton 131
Café Truva 136
Caffeine 115
Circus Café 131
Elephant House 25, 98
Favorit 98
Fruitmarket Gallery Café 35, 108
Gallery Café, The 131
Glass & Thompson 35, 116
Kaffe Politik 149
Luca, S. 17, 149
Number 28, 116
Palace of Holyroodhouse Café 89
Palm Court 104, 108
Plaisir du Chocolat 44, 78
Queen Street Café 116
Relish 136
Spoon 78
Stables Tearoom 155
Starbucks Coffee 109
Terrace Café 127, 131
Valvona & Crolla 38, 124
Caledonian Beer Festival 47, 141, 180
Caledonian Brewery 47, 140, 144, 180
Caley Sample Room 144
Calton Hill 120
Calton Hill 10, 32, 47, 48, 51, 57, 61, 119–125, 180
Calton Old Burial Ground 23, 119
camera obscura 70
Canongate Kirk 20, 76
Canongate Tolbooth 75
Capital Christmas 47, 105, 181
car parking 181
car rental 181
Castle Esplanade 69
Castle, Edinburgh 11, 14, 50, 67
Charlie, Bonnie Prince 67, 110
Charlotte Square 112
Children's Festival 180
cinemas 175
City Art Centre 105
City Chambers 74
City Observatory 121
Clifford, Timothy 107
climate 4
climbing, indoor 29, 52, 143
clubs 40, 43, 171
coaches 171
comedy venues 41, 175
Conan Doyle, Sir Arthur 96, 122
Corstorphine Hill 139
Craig, James 76, 110, 121
Craigmillar Castle 145
Cramond 60, 142

Customs House 135
cycle tours 170

d

Dalhousie Castle 45, 167
Dalmeny House 152
Dalmeny station 151
Dance Base 55, 92, 175
dance venues 174
Darwin, Charles 139
Dean Bridge 128
Dean Gallery 27, 63, 130, 131
Dean Village 8, 37, 126, 128
Discovery Room, The 111
doggerfisher 123
Doors Open Day 179
drinking 30
Duddingston Loch 88
Duddingston village 31, 88
Dunbar's Close Garden 37, 76
Dundas Street 27, 113
Dynamic Earth 53, 86

e

Edinburgh Book Festival 113, 178
Edinburgh Castle 11, 14, 50, 67
Edinburgh Dungeon 104
Edinburgh Festival 12, 176–179
Edinburgh International Airport 171
Edinburgh Military Tattoo 70, 179
Edinburgh Printmakers Gallery 123
Edinburgh Zoo 53, 139
eighty shilling (80/-) ale 17
Elm Row pigeons 63
entertainment 172
Esplanade, Castle 69

f

Family History Centre 102
Fergusson, Robert 76
ferries 171
Festival, Edinburgh 12, 176–179
Festival Theatre 19, 175
Film Festival 178
Filmhouse 97, 175
Fire Festival 47, 180

fish and chips 17, 79
Fishmarket Close 55
flights 171, 181
Flotterstone 148
food and drink 16, 34, 38
football 180
Forth Bridges 10, 61, 151–156
Forth Bridges 152
Fringe, Edinburgh Festival 13, 175
Fruitmarket Gallery 26, 35, 104, 108

g

Gallery of Modern Art 63, 128, 131
gay clubs and bars 172
gay scene 7, 42, 122, 124, 125, 174, 180, 182
genealogical research 22, 102, 182
General Register House 22, 102
George Heriot's School 93
Georgian House, The 33, 113
ghost tours 23, 67, 92
Gladstone's Land 21, 71, 159
Glenkinchie whisky 17
Goldsworthy, Andy 62, 94, 127
golf 29, 133, 145, 150, 182
Grassmarket 21, 90
graveyard tours 67, 92
Great Michael 136
Greyfriars Bobby statue 23, 93
Greyfriars Kirk 92
guesthouses 159–167
gun, one o'clock 69, 121

h

Hamilton, Thomas 119
Hare, William 92, 96
Haymarket Station 171
Heart of Midlothian 73
Heriot Row 112
Heriot, George 93
Hermitage of Braid 147
High Kirk of St Giles 15, 21, 73
Hilland 148
Hogmanay 46, 181
Holmes, Sherlock 96, 122
Holyrood 84
Holyrood 82–89
Holyrood Abbey 20, 83
Holyrood Park 8, 49, 87

Holyroodhouse, Palace of 15, 82, 89
Honours of Scotland 14
Hopetoun House 32, 153, 155
hospital 182
hostels 167
hotels 159–167
Hub, The 71
Hume, David 119
Hutton, James 87

i

ice cream 17, 149
Inchcolm Island 154
information 172
Ingleby Gallery 120
internet cafés 182
Inverleith 8
Inverleith House 127
Irn Bru 16, 149

j

James IV 133, 136
James VI 14, 95
Jazz and Blues Festival 179
Jencks, Charles 63, 128
John Knox's House 75

k

Kemp, George Meikle 106
kids' Edinburgh 52
kilts 77, 136
King's Wark 138
Knights of the Thistle 15, 73
Knox, John 73, 75

l

Lady Stair's House 72
Laurison Castle 141
law courts 72
left luggage 180
Leith 134
Leith 7, 61, 133–138
Leith Links 133
Leith Walk 63
Lister, Joseph 96
literary pub tour 25
literature 24
live music venues 174
Loony Dook 28, 152, 180
Lorimer, Sir Robert 73
lost property 182

m

Maid of the Forth 154
Makars' Court 72
Mansfield Place Church 123
Mary King's Close 37, 74
Mary, Queen of Scots 14, 15, 67, 75, 82, 83, 110, 146
Meadows, The 49, 145
Medieval Edinburgh 20
Mela, The Edinburgh 179
Mendelssohn, Felix 83
Merz 123
Military Tattoo 70, 179
Mining Museum 53, 149
Miralles, Enric 55, 85, 107
modern art 62
Mons Meg 69
Moray Place 112
Mound, The 106, 107
Murrayfield Stadium 141, 180
Museum of Childhood 74
Museum of Edinburgh 75
Museum of Scotland 11, 27, 54, 93, 98, 100
music 18
music venues 174

n

National Archives of Scotland 22, 102
National Covenant 75, 92
National Gallery of Scotland 27, 33, 88, 106, 109, 180
National Library of Scotland 22, 90
National Monument, Calton Hill 32, 57, 121
National Museum of Scotland 11, 27, 54, 93, 98, 100
National Trust for Scotland 33, 71, 113, 116
National War Memorial 69
Nelson Monument 61, 121
Ness 77
New Register House 102
New Town 111
New Town 7, 33, 110–118
New Year's Eve 46, 181
Newhaven 136
Newhaven Heritage Museum 136
nightclubs 40, 43, 173
North and west Edinburgh 140
North Bridge 81

o

Observatory, City 121
Observatory, Royal 146
Ocean Terminal 135, 136, 175
Old College 95
Old Royal High School 119
Old Town 7
Omni Centre 122, 175
One O'clock Gun 69, 121
One Spa 45
Open Eye Gallery 114
opening hours 182
Our Dynamic Earth 53, 86
Outlook Tower 70
oysters 39

p

Palace of Holyroodhouse 15, 82, 89
Paolozzi, Sir Eduardo 27, 63, 94, 122, 130
Parliament, New Scottish 11, 55, 72, 84, 120
Parliament Square 21, 72
penguin parade 139
Pentland Hills 147
People's Story, The 75
pharmacies 180
Phoenix 369 gallery 114
Picardy Place 122
Pigeon sculptures 63
Playfair Library 95
Playfair, William 95, 96, 107, 108, 121
Poetry Library 76
police 180
Portrait Gallery 56, 110, 116
post office 182
Potter, Harry 25, 98
Pride Scotia festival 42, 180
Princes Street 103
Princes Street 102–109
Princes Street Gardens 47, 49, 105
pub tour, literary 25
public transport 171
pubs and bars (by area)
  Along Princes Street 109
  Along the Water of Leith 132
  Calton Hill and Broughton 125
  Holyrood and Arthur's Seat 89
  Leith 138
  New Town 118
  North and west Edinburgh 143
  Royal Mile 80
  South Edinburgh 150
  South of the Royal Mile 100

South Queensferry and the
Forth Bridges 156
pubs and bars
  Assembly 100
  Athletic Bar 144
  Bailie Bar 132
  Bar Java 138
  Barony Bar, The 125
  Basement, The 125
  Bert's Bar 132
  Black Bo's 80
  Blue Blazer 100
  Bow Bar 30, 100
  Café Royal Circle Bar 30, 109
  Caley Sample Room 144
  Cramond Inn 144
  Cumberland Bar 31, 118
  Deacon Brodie's Tavern 80
  Diggers, The (Athletic Arms)
    144
  Dome, The 40, 118
  EH1 80
  Fishtank 41, 118
  Greyfriars Bobby Bar 92, 100
  Hamiltons Bar and Kitchen
    132
  Hawes Inn 156
  Human Be-In 41
  Jolly Judge 31, 81
  King's Wark 138
  Last Drop Tavern 23, 100
  North Bridge 81
  Opal Lounge 41, 118
  Outhouse 125
  Oxford Bar 25, 118
  Pivo 125
  Planet Out 43, 125, 174
  Sala 174
  Sandy Bell's 19
  Sheep Heid Inn 31, 88, 89
  Shore Bar 31, 138
  Traverse Bar Café 101
  Tun Bar, The 89
  Valvona & Crolla VinCaffè 118
  Villager 101

q

Queen's Drive 87
Queen's Gallery 15, 83
Queensferry Museum 152

r

Raeburn Place 127
railway services 171, 172
Ramsay Gardens 70
Randolph Gallery 114
Rankin, Ian 25, 118
Ratho Adventure Centre 29,
  52, 143
Rebus, Inspector 25, 118
reformation 73, 75

Reid, Robert 72
restaurants (by area)
  Along Princes Street 109
  Along the Water of Leith 131
  Calton Hill and Broughton 124
  Holyrood and Arthur's Seat 89
  Leith 137
  New Town 116
  North and west Edinburgh
    143
  Royal Mile 79
  South Edinburgh 150
  South of the Royal Mile 99
  South Queensferry and the
    Forth Bridges 156
restaurants
  Amber 79
  Apartment 150
Atrium 99
  Barioja 79
  Bell's Diner 131
  blue 99
  Blue Parrot Cantina 132
  Boathouse 156
  Britannia Spice 137
  Café Royal Oyster Bar 109
  Café St Honoré 116
  Centotre 116
  Clamshell 79
  Cuisine d'Odile, La 116
  Daniel's 137
  David Bann's 34, 79
  Dionika 132
  Doric Tavern 109
  Dusit 117
  Erawan Oriental 89
  Fishers 34, 137
  Fishers in the City 117
  Forth Floor Restaurant 117
  Gallery Restaurant 109
  Grain Store, The 35, 99
  Hadrian's Brasserie 104
  Henderson's Salad Table 117
  Howies at Waterloo 124
  La Garrigue 79
  Lancers 132
  Le Sept 80
  Maison Bleue 99
  Malmaison Brasserie 137
  Mussel Inn 117
  Namaste 99
  New Bell, The 150
  No. 3 Royal Terrace 124
  Number One 104, 109
  Off the Wall 80
  Oloroso 51, 117
  Orocco Pier 156
  Outsider, The 99
  Petit Paris 100
  Pizza Express 132
  Prego 80
  Rapido 125
  Reform restaurant 80
  Restaurant Martin Wishart
    45, 137
  Room in the Town 118
  Room in the West End 144
  Scotch Whisky Heritage

  Centre 79
  Shore Restaurant 137
  Skerries Seafood Restau-
    rant 143
  Songkran 144
  Stac Polly 118
  Stockbridge Restaurant 132
  Stone Room 143
  Suruchi 100
  Sweet Melinda's 150
  Thai Me Up in Edinburgh 125
  Thaisanuk 150
  Tower 35, 94, 100
  Vintners' Rooms 138
  Viva Mexico 80
  Waterfront Wine Bar 138
  Witchery by the Castle 37, 80
River Almond 60, 142
Ross Bandstand 105
Rosslyn Chapel 57, 148
Rosyth ferry terminal 171
Rowling, J.K. 25, 98
Royal Botanic Garden 48, 51,
  62, 126, 131
Royal Highland Show 47, 180
Royal Lyceum Theatre 97,
  175
Royal Mile 68
Royal Mile 11, 67–81
Royal Museum of Scotland
  26, 94, 98
Royal Observatory 146
Royal Scottish Academy 107
Royal Yacht Britannia 7, 14,
  15, 61, 135
rugby 29, 141, 178

s

St Andrew Square coach and
  bus station 171, 172
St Andrew's Day 181
St Andrew's House 119
St Bernard's Well 33, 126
St Giles, High Kirk of 15,
  21, 73
St James Centre 122
St Margaret's Chapel 69
St Mary's Roman Catholic
  Cathedral 122
St Stephen Street 59, 127
Salisbury Crags 8, 51, 87
Science Festival 180
Scotch Whisky Heritage Cen-
  tre 70, 79
Scott Monument 106
Scott, Sir Walter 24, 72, 106
Scottish Gallery 114
Scottish Mining Museum
  53, 149
Scottish National Gallery of
  Modern Art 63, 128, 131

Scottish National Portrait Gallery 56, 110, 116
Scottish Parliament 11, 55, 72, 84, 120
Scottish Poetry Library 76
Scottish Storytelling Centre 75
self-catering apartments 159–167
shops (by area)
Along Princes Street 108
Along the Water of Leith 131
Calton Hill and Broughton 123
Leith 136
New Town 114
North and west Edinburgh 143
Royal Mile 77
shops
Annie Smith 131
Anta 59, 97
Blackwell's 97
Cadenhead's Whisky Shop 77
Carson Clark Map Gallery 77
Coda 77
Concrete Butterfly 97
Corniche 58, 77
Crombies 123
Cruise 115
Fabhatrix 97
Farmers' Market 39, 97
Flux 136
Geoffrey (Tailor) Kiltmakers 77
Harvey Nichols 59, 115
Helen Bateman Shoes 143
Herbie of Edinburgh 131
Iain Mellis Cheesemonger 39, 97, 131
InHouse 115
Jane Davidson 115
Jenners 58, 108
Joey D 124
Joseph Bonnar 114
Just Scottish 78
Kinloch Anderson 136
Luca, S. 17, 149
McAlister Matheson Music 97
McNaughtan's Bookshop 25, 124
National Museum of Scotland Shop 98
Ness 77
Ocean Terminal 136
Plaisir du Chocolat 44
Ragamuffin 78
Relish 136
St Stephen Street shops 59

Tiso 115
Valvona & Crolla 38, 124
Victoria Street shops 21, 59, 97
Villeneuve Wines 124
Waterstone's 108, 109
William Cadenhead 39
Wm. Armstrong 98
Shore, The 61, 134
Simpson, Sir James Young 96, 111
skating 47, 105
skiing, dry-slope 148
Smith, Adam 76
South Edinburgh 146
South of the Royal Mile 91
South Queensferry 28, 61, 151–156
South Queensferry 152
spas 45
sports and activities 28
Stevenson, Robert Louis 25, 72, 80, 156
Stockbridge 8, 126, 127
Stone of Destiny (Stone of Scone) 69
Surgeons' Hall Museum 22, 57, 96
swimming pools 180

Talbot Rice Art Gallery 95
Tattoo 70, 177
taxis 170
Telford, Thomas 128
theatreland 97
theatres 172
Thistle Chapel, High Kirk of St Giles 15, 73
tipping 180
Torrance Gallery 114
tourist office 170
tours 23, 36, 67, 92, 170
trains 171
transport 171
Traquair, Phoebe Anna 123
Traverse Theatre 19, 97, 101, 173
Trinity Apse church 74
Trinity House 133

underground vaults 36
University of Edinburgh 95, 163
Usher Hall 19, 97, 172

Victoria Street shops 21, 59, 97
Victoria Swing Bridge 135

walking tours 67, 170
War Memorial 69
Water of Leith 128
Water of Leith 8, 33, 37, 49, 126–132
Water of Leith walkway 8, 37, 126, 128
Waverley novels 106
Waverley station 102, 104, 105, 171
weather 4
websites 170
Weston Link 107
whisky 17, 39, 70, 79, 100
Whisky Heritage Centre 70, 79
William Cadenhead 39, 77
Witches' Fountain 70
World City of Literature 24
World Heritage Site 4, 110
Writers' Museum 72

youth hostels 167–168

Zoo 53, 139